AC/DC

THE EARLY YEARS WITH BON SCOTT

D1393192

Published in 2013 by
INDEPENDENT MUSIC PRESS
Independent Music Press is an imprint of I.M. P. Publishing Limited
This Work is Copyright © I. M. P. Publishing Ltd 2012

AC/DC – The Early Years With Bon Scott
by Neil Daniels

British Library Cataloguing-in-Publication Data.
A catalogue for this book is available from The British Library.
ISBN: 978-1-906191-24-5
Cover Design by Fresh Lemon.
Cover photo by Brian Rasic/Rex Features

Independent Music Press
P.O. Box 69,
Church Stretton, Shropshire
SY6 6WZ
Visit us on the web at: www.impbooks.com
For a free catalogue, e-mail us at: info@impbooks.com

AC/DC

*The Early Years
With Bon Scott*

by Neil Daniels

Independent Music Press

DEDICATED TO

RONALD BELFORD SCOTT
(ALSO KNOWN AS BON SCOTT)

JULY 9, 1946 – FEBRUARY 19, 1980

CONTENTS

PART I:
THE EARLY YEARS

FOREWORD BY MICK BOX (URIAH HEEP)

Well, what can be said about AC/DC that has not already been said?!

They are one of the most influential hard rock bands of the 1970s, and their kind of driving rock gave the power chord a whole new meaning. Their sound was in essence minimalist, which gave it even more power and on top of this mammoth power chord roar for the early part of their career was Bon Scott's larynx-shredding vocals. They took their brand of bar-room rock from the pubs and clubs in Sydney, Australia into the biggest arenas in the world and nobody does it better. From the count of four on the high-hat, the head banging starts and it never lets up.

As flattering as it may seem, many bands have imitated them, but they do not even get close, as AC/DC have perfected riffs and songs that have truly stood the test of time that everyone still loves to hear in the live arena, even to this day.

Throughout their career they have lyrically favoured double entendres, but this was always done with a mischievous sense of fun. From their first albums – *High Voltage* (recorded in 1974, released in 1975) and *T.N.T.* in 1975 – they had set the template that has taken them on to being one of (if not the biggest) rock bands in the world!

AC/DC

Angus as a guitarist is phenomenal, and he has what seems to be a limitless amount of energy on stage, but he is only allowed this freedom to shine by the rock solid performance of the others. Each one of them plays their part perfectly, and this produces a brand of infectious rock music like no other.

The perfect way to finish this foreword is to quote their eighth Australian, and seventh international studio album, released in 1981, *For Those About To Rock We Salute You*, and if rock music is your genre of choice, then you can do no better than rock out with AC/DC.

'Appy days!

Mick Box
Uriah Heep
www.uriah-heep.com

INTRODUCTION

AC/DC are now rightfully regarded as one of the world's greatest rock bands. Despite the periods of critical ridicule they have suffered throughout much of their career it is only recently that they have started to earn the reverence that is long overdue. They've sold 200 million albums worldwide, and despite long breaks in between albums throughout the past twenty years, they continue to sell millions of records every year.

It can be argued that there are several distinct phases to AC/DC's career which began in 1973 in Sydney, Australia. There is the Dave Evans period; the band's original frontman. The Evans era was then followed by the Bon Scott years, beginning in 1974, which took the band right up to his untimely death in 1980 (some argue this was the band's creative heyday). Following that phase, there's the start of the Brian Johnson years with 1980's *Back In Black* and 1981's *For Those About To Rock We Salute You*, both of which were produced by Robert 'Mutt' Lange; this particular phase ended in 1983 with the departure of drummer Phil Rudd. The band then entered what many feel was a creative decline for several years though they continued to be a major live draw, but it wasn't until 1990's *The Razor's Edge* that they got close to the brilliance of their earlier work along with chart success, high sales and decent reviews. With Phil Rudd back in the fold in the mid-1990s, the band entered a new phase with the *Back In Black* line-up of lead guitarist Angus Young, rhythm guitarist Malcolm Young, bassist Cliff Williams, drummer Phil Rudd and singer Brian Johnson. This phase saw them release

AC/DC

1995's *Ballbreaker* and 2000's *Stiff Upper Lip* and though they had clearly slowed down their output, they continued to commit themselves to lengthy world tours every few years. It seemed like they had left the creative decline of the mid–1980s behind them and were back on top form which is why 2008's *Black Ice* saw the band enter a new phase altogether. Armed with *Black Ice*, arguably one of their finest albums to date, AC/DC have perhaps become more popular than ever before.

However, such discussions are required for another book because – as the title suggests – this particular work is about the Bon Scott years of 1974 to 1979, although the author has taken the obvious liberty of including a chapter about the Dave Evans period as well as a chapter detailing the success of *Back In Black*, which was released essentially as a tribute to the late Bon Scott. Also included is a postscript that chronicles Bon Scott-related posthumous releases and a chapter in the appendix that can be used as a chronology of the band's albums released after the singer's death, which also places the critical and commercial successes of the Bon Scott years into perspective.

AC/DC were clearly on a creative high during the Bon Scott era. It was obvious from the release of their first international album *High Voltage* in 1976 (which was a compilation of the two Aussie-released albums *High Voltage* (1975) and *T.N.T.* (1975)), that they were going to be a very special band indeed, even though many critics thought they were trite. 1976's entertaining *Dirty Deeds Done Dirt Cheap*, 1977's masterful *Let There Be Rock*, 1978's electrifying *Powerage*, the now classic 1978 live album *If You Want Blood You've Got It* and 1979's legendary *Highway To Hell* show the band's quick and steady progression from a fledgling club rock band to a devastatingly brilliant professional hard rock act of world-class prowess.

Bon Scott was utterly unique and it was his originality, charm, idiosyncracies and showmanship (amongst other traits) that helped propel the band from the grimy clubs of Eastern Australia to the famous venues of Europe and the USA. The band carried on after his death not only in his memory but also because they knew he'd want them to carry on the AC/DC name.

The Early Years is not about the death of Bon Scott, which has been extensively written about in numerous tomes and in countless articles on the band, but a celebration of the music and a tribute to one of rock's finest frontmen.

Like the author's previous book on the early years of Metallica, *AC/DC – The Early Years With Bon Scott* charts not only the rise of the band but also offers a chronology and analysis of every album they made with Bon Scott. Of course, there is an entire library of books on AC/DC and numerous others, but this is not a biography *per se* as it concentrates on a specific time-frame in their career and focuses on the music as opposed to the personal lives of the band. *The Early Years With Bon Scott* is not an exhaustive biography; it is a casual, easily digestible guide to the music and tours within a certain era.

The story of Bon Scott is ultimately a tragic one given his premature death, but let's not wallow on the sad times and instead embrace the fantastic music that was made between 1974, when he joined the band, and 1980 when he died. When a rock star dies young there is often a tendency to sensationalise the details with little regard for the music and the talent that made the person a star in the first place. In this book, Bon's music will be detailed, not his death. His music will live on far beyond the tragic details of his death. Let us remember not events leading to his premature death, but his stage presence, his music and his legacy.

And of course, *AC/DC* – we salute them!

Neil Daniels
www.neildaniels.com
neildanielsbooks.wordpress.com

THE DAVE EVANS ERA
1973-1974

"Look, I was with the band from the first rehearsal through to the day we split – every day. But that was only a year or so and we had our differences even during that time."

Dave Evans speaking to Simon Rushworth
of *Rush On Rock* in 2010

On December 9, 1979, AC/DC played a truly mesmerising performance at the Pavillon de Paris in Paris, France, in front of several thousand hardcore rock fans. Although the band's performances were relatively short back in those days at around eighty minutes, the sheer amount of energy, charisma and prowess AC/DC displayed was simply staggering. The concert was released theatrically – and later on VHS and DVD – and watching it now, over twenty years later, it's amazing just how much impact this line-up of AC/DC – singer Bon Scott, lead guitarist Angus Young, rhythm guitarist Malcolm Young, bassist Cliff Williams and drummer Phil Rudd – continues to have on rock fans and new generations of bands the world over. The concert – released as *Let There Be Rock: The Movie, Live In Paris* – is an important historical document and a fine tribute to the Bon Scott years but of course AC/DC started out as something entirely different...

AC/DC was formed by Scottish-born brothers Malcolm and Angus Young in November 1973 with singer Dave Evans,

AC/DC

American-born bassist Larry Van Kriedt and drummer Colin Burgess. Malcolm was the driving force behind the band.

Malcolm Young was born Malcolm Mitchell Young on January 6, 1953 in Glasgow, to William and Margaret Young. The Youngs lived in the Cranhill area of Glasgow, a working-class housing estate that was erected in the 1950s to cope with the post-war housing shortage. Situated on the east end of Glasgow and comprising mostly of tower blocks of flats often dubbed "high flats", it was a publically funded area and many of the families that lived there were poor and/or unemployed. However, much of Glasgow was destitute and the housing conditions that Cranhill offered was a stark contrast to the notorious Glasgow slums. In May, 1963, the Youngs – William and Margaret with their three boys George, Malcolm, Angus and their sister Margaret – uprooted and moved to Sydney, Australia. There is another Young offspring who is less often heard of: Alex Young – the oldest of the four lads – who stayed in Scotland after the rest of his family emigrated. Alex headed down to London to form and play bass in Grapefruit with Tony Rivers and Pete and Geoff Swettenham.

AC/DC's second Young brother and Malcolm's closest ally, Angus, was born Angus McKinnon Young on March 31, 1955, the youngest of the children. Angus's first instrument was a banjo which he soon restrung to make a six-stringer. Angus was a big fan of Little Richard as a kid and his influences included Chuck Berry, Freddie King, John Lee Hooker, Jimi Hendrix and The Kinks. Both Malcolm and Angus loved the way the white English players of the 1960s took the pre- and immediate post-war blues sound and merged it with rock 'n' roll to create a heavy, authentic and truly electrifying brand of music that would eventually lead the way for hard rock and heavy metal. The way the likes of Robert Johnson, Buddy Guy, Muddy Waters, Elmore James, Howlin' Wolf, John Lee Hooker, B.B. King and so many more guitarists played and sung the blues had a tremendous impact on Jimmy Page, Eric Clapton, Jeff Beck and all the other British guitarists of the 1960s. Ironically, those African-American blues players were relatively obscure in their homeland and it wasn't until the British bands of the 1960s that many Americans would rightfully, albeit belatedly, acknowledge their existence.

Angus was mesmerised by the sounds of Jimi Hendrix; the way Hendrix played his Fender Stratocaster and his use of amplified feedback was awe-inspiring. Cream, and later The Who and Led Zeppelin, were the first bands to "Go West" and exploit the lucrative American market. They travelled thousands of miles around the USA playing all manner of venues and to all kinds of audiences. British bands ventured to the USA and soaked up American culture and visited parts of the Deep South that inspired the African-American blues players. Many of said bands were in awe of American music; it was the fusion of blues, jazz, folk, rockabilly and soul that created the hard blues rock sounds of the 1960s, hence the term "British Blues Boom".

Actually Angus didn't think the guitar was such a big deal until he reached his teens and ended up with a Hofner guitar and an amplifier worth sixty Australian dollars. The amplifier didn't go down well with everyone, given Angus's fondness for playing loudly! He once played a gig at a local church as a fill-in for a guitarist who'd dropped out of some local band and Angus ended up getting complaints from members of the audience who said it was just too bloody loud. Around 1967, Angus bought a dark brown second-hand Gibson SG from a music store in Sydney and in so doing his future was set. Given Angus's latterday frenetic on-stage persona, the light-weight Gibson was perfect for him. He learned that the Fender model was just a little bit too heavy for his small frame. Angus didn't read or understand music and initially as a teenager he didn't have a clue about chord playing and structure; like many musicians of his generation he made up his own riffs and soloing was a pretty easy endeavour for him. It was his elder brother Malcolm who taught him about chords.

Both Angus and Malcolm stayed close to their Scots roots despite the massive geographical distance by supporting their beloved football team, Glasgow Rangers. After moving around, the Youngs finally made a home for themselves in Burwood, a leafy and pleasant suburb of Sydney that proved to be a comfortable environment for their family.

AC/DC

Perhaps the biggest influence on Malcolm and Angus at the time they were just learning about music was their older sibling George (born George Redburn Young on November 6, 1946 in Bridgeton, Glasgow) who was the first Young offspring to pick up a guitar. George Young joined The Easybeats, one of Australia's most prominent bands, between 1964 and 1969. They scored a hit in 1966 with the infectious track, 'Friday On My Mind'. In fact, they were one of the first Australian bands to have an international hit and said track remains a classic Australian pop song. George was an integral member of The Easybeats and co-wrote many of their songs, initially with singer Steve Wright and later, lead guitarist Harry Vanda.

Vanda (short for Vandenberg; his full name is Johannes Hendricus Jacob Vandenberg) was born in The Netherlands in 1946, so like the Youngs he was a migrant rather than an Australian native. Both the Youngs and the Vandenbergs lived at the Villawood Migrant Hostel in Sydney in 1963; soon thereafter The Easybeats was formed with fellow migrants singer Steve Wright, bassist Dick Diamonde and drummer Gordon Fleet with lead guitarist Harry Vanda and rhythm guitarist George Young completing the line-up.

In 2007, *Australian Musician* declared that the meeting of George Young and Harry Vanda at that Sydney hostel in 1964 was one of the most important events in Australian music history. Vanda and Young became songwriting partners in 1966 after The Easybeats had signed with EMI. They travelled to the UK and USA and ventured all over Australia too, such was their success as pop songwriters. In 1970, Vanda and Young would form a songwriting and production partnership after The Easybeats folded the previous year. They moved to the UK for a couple of years where they wrote and recorded various tracks under different names before moving back to Australia in 1973.

Looking at the success of George Young, Malcolm was enthused enough to pick up a guitar and play in a band called Velvet Underground in Newcastle, New South Wales (not to be confused with Loud Reed's former New York rock band). Malcolm and Angus saw George infrequently when they were kids because their elder sibling's success meant he was always working and on the road but they certainly admired him and ultimately he would have a fundamental impact on his younger brothers. Velvet Underground mostly churned out covers of songs by T-Rex and the Rolling Stones. Malcolm was a huge blues fan and was primarily influenced by the white English blues guitarists and bands of the 1960s such as The Yardbirds, The Kinks and Cream as well as the 1950s American rock 'n' roll stars like Eddie Cochran and Carl Perkins. The Youngs tended to favour artists that played the blues rather than, say, the early pop sound of The Beatles or the other Merseybeat bands. There was something about the blues that utterly fascinated Malcolm and Angus; it was clear that the blues was going to play a major part in their musical careers, even at this early age.

At the time of Velvet Underground, Malcolm's kid brother Angus was jamming in a band called Kantuckee. The first line-up of Kantuckee featured Bob McGlynn on vocals, Jon Stevens on bass, drummer Trevor James and Angus. The band folded then regrouped under the moniker Tantrum with singer-guitarist Mark Sneddon, Jon Stevens on bass, Trevor James on drums and Angus on guitar. Ultimately these bands didn't break through but they provided good training grounds for both guitarists.

Soon Malcolm and Angus felt could find success by forming a band themselves and working together. Whose idea was it for them to join forces? "Malcolm was putting together a band," Angus remembered in an interview with Paul Cashmere of *Undercover* in 2008. "He found a condemned building in Newtown [Australia] and said he could get it for a couple of bucks. He was just auditioning guys and telling people to come down and try-out. A week later he said to me, 'Why don't you bring your guitar down and try out?' I thought, *Great, anything but a day job.*"

Thus AC/DC was founded in November, 1973 by Malcolm (then twenty years old) and his eighteen-year-old brother. AC/DC was instantly a taut family unit and the Young brothers' older sister Margaret also had an integral role to play in the early years of the band. Margaret would take Malcolm and Angus to

AC/DC

concerts in Sydney, opening their minds to new worlds of music; they went to see The Beatles and even jazz legend Louis Armstrong. A popular venue for music-loving Sydney residents was Sydney Stadium which used to attract the biggest artists of the day.

They needed a band moniker very quickly as they had hooked up with a booking agency in Sydney that already had some gigs planned for them before the end of the year. According to some sources, it was also Margaret's idea to name the band AC/DC after she saw the initials on a sewing machine. AC/DC is an abbreviation of alternating current/direct current and what better name for a raw and energetic rock 'n' roll band? However, other reports suggest that it was George Young's wife Sandra who came up with the idea of naming the band AC/DC. The band's official site states that the name was 'taken from the power outlet on the family vacuum cleaner.' Whatever the original source of the idea, the name was perfect.

The Young brothers set about recruiting other musicians to fill the slots in their new band. Bassist Larry Van Kriedt (born 1954, who to this day remains the only member in AC/DC's history to have been born in the USA) moved to Sydney in 1969 and met the Young brothers not long after settling in Australia. Coming from a jazz-influenced background, Kriedt – whose father David Van Kriedt was a successful jazz musician – appeared to have little in common musically with Malcolm and Angus Young whose influences were solely blues and rock 'n' roll, but they got on well so they invited him to join their new band. Van Kriedt was very talented which must have appealed to the two Scots lads: he could play bass, double bass and saxophone. The band also recruited drummer Colin Burgess (born November 16, 1946) who had previously played in the cult Aussie band, The Masters Apprentices from 1968 to 1972.

The first line-up of AC/DC consisted of Angus Young on lead guitar, Malcolm Young on rhythm guitar, Colin Burgess on drums, Larry Van Kriedt on bass and singer Dave Evans (born July 20, 1963). Malcolm drafted in Evans from his old band Velvet Underground (though the pair had not actually been in the band together, because by the time Evans joined Velvet Underground, Malcolm had already left to form AC/DC with his brother).

In 2007, Evans spoke to Mark Prindle of *Citizine* about his introduction to AC/DC after the demise of Velvet Underground: "I heard a knock on the door a little bit later on, and Angus Young was there. I hadn't heard of Angus. He introduced himself as the younger brother of Malcolm, and his band Kantuckee was looking for a singer and he had heard of me through the grapevine. But the music that they were playing was very heavily guitar-oriented music; there weren't a lot of vocals involved in the stuff that they were doing at the time, so I declined that. Then not long after that I did actually answer an ad in the *Sydney Morning Herald* for a heavy rock singer. And it was Malcolm Young!"

Malcolm gave Evans the low-down on the band and explained that he'd hired Colin Burgess and Larry Van Kriedt. Evans met up with the three of them in the Sydney suburb of Newtown, and they jammed together and sounded good. They got on well and had a laugh and not long after the session Malcolm told Evans that his younger brother Angus was in a band that had just split-up and that he was also going to audition for them. Angus joined the four of them at their next jam session and the five musicians gelled well.

The one integral connection between Evans and the Young brothers was their shared infatuation with the blues. Evans' favourite singer was the young Paul Rodgers of Free from the North-East of England and his other favourite band was Led Zeppelin. Evans' other influences included The Beatles, the Rolling Stones, The Troggs and Deep Purple. Evans, however, had an entirely different upbringing from the Young brothers and there was certainly a culture clash between the two sides.

"Angus and Malcolm were still living at home with their parents and were part of a very close and supportive family," Dave Evans explained to R. Scott Bolton of *Rough Edge* in 2006. "I had left home at sixteen after a huge row with my father over my long hair and had headed for Kings Cross in Sydney which was a pretty rough environment. Although it was the gambling, drugs and prostitution centre of Sydney, it was also where many aspiring artists and musicians lived. It was quite an experience and a place where at times it was heaven and other times it was hell. I grew up in a hurry and was quite a wild young man in those days."

The band began playing live and with the help of Australian roadie Ray Arnold and his partner Alan Kissack, they managed to enthuse the entertainment manager (Gene Pierson) of a prominent Sydney night spot – Chequers – to allow the band to play there on New Year's Eve, 1973. However, AC/DC were loud. *Very* loud. So much so that there were complaints about the volume.

There was some hype around the show as word of mouth had spread that the two younger brothers of The Easybeats' George Young were in the band and the Masters Apprentices' Colin Burgess was also involved. It was their first gig and what better place than Sydney's top nightspot? The new band was bound to attract good-sized audiences in time to come given the relentless energy and charisma they'd displayed in their first performance in front of a crowd. The show went down well but like any other ambitious and hard-working band just starting out they would quickly improve.

The band went through a number of line-up changes at this very early point: Larry Van Kriedt (who'd only been in the band for four months) was briefly succeeded by Neil Smith in February 1974 although by April, Smith had left and been replaced by Rob Bailey whose previous bands included Acid Road, Rudy and the Aardvarks, and Natural Gas who supported the Rolling Stones in 1972 and 1973. Also, drummer Colin Burgess was then replaced and shortly after Larry would also depart; the band's early line-up was very fluid and at times difficult to follow.

Burgess was replaced more permanently by Peter Clack who joined in April after brief spots on the drum stool by Ron Carpenter, Russell Coleman and Noel Taylor. Peter Clack's previous band was named Flake, which also featured bassist Rob Bailey. Between April and September 1974 the line-up of

AC/DC was: lead guitarist Angus Young, rhythm guitarist Malcolm Young, singer Dave Evans, drummer Peter Clack and bassist Rob Bailey.

Like most rock 'n' roll bands that have an impact on popular culture, AC/DC needed an image or an icon and after the group started playing live, Angus Young began to experiment with stage clothes: he tried a Zorro uniform, a Spider-Man costume, a gorilla and even a Superman spoof which he comically dubbed "Super-Ang". None of them really worked. They needed something that would stand out, something truly unique and individual that would cement itself in the minds of fans and make people think of AC/DC whenever they saw the image. Other ideas included wearing crash helmets and even having the drummer dressed as a court jester but needless to say they didn't materialise (thankfully).

The idea for Angus to wear a school uniform came from his older sister, Margaret. She'd always remembered Angus running around the house after school with his guitar strapped on whilst he was still wearing his uniform, so she said he should wear that in the band as it would give the people something to look at; something to remember. The band even tried their hand at creating a publicity stunt by telling the media that Angus was born in 1959 rather than 1955 thus giving him the age of a schoolboy. The first uniform he wore onstage was actually from his secondary high school, Ashfield Boys High School in Sydney. Not only would Angus's schoolboy uniform become an iconic part of the band's image but in time he would mimic and parody Chuck Berry's already famous duckwalk.

Dave Evans remembered the first time Angus dressed as a schoolboy at Sydney's Victoria Park in April, 1974 when Neil Smith and Noel Taylor were (briefly) in the band. Evans said to Mark Prindle of *Citizine* in 2007, "He played hard and he had a lot of energy, but he didn't really do much [in terms of stage antics], no. And at the Victoria Park show I was completely taken aback, because once he had this schoolboy uniform on, he just ripped up the stage! He was running and jumping up and down. I remember thinking to myself, 'Boy, this is *fantastic!*' So that

Angus in his new genuine schoolboy uniform.
Courtesy of Chris Capstick/Rex Features

schoolboy uniform really did something to his psyche and shaped what he does. He's a fantastic performer. But up until then, he wasn't a great performer. But that schoolboy uniform certainly did something to him, because he started ripping the place up."

It was Malcolm who brought Angus forward to the front of the stage, telling him he needed to be more active. Angus was very shy back then, previously just standing still playing the guitar but when he put that schoolboy uniform on he'd become somebody completely different. Standing still didn't exactly work in Angus's favour anyway; he was a stationary target for the drunks and hecklers that frequented the clubs and pubs AC/DC played in back then.

The Victoria Park concert was a major coup for the band because it was a large outdoor venue that attracted thousands of music fans. The gig has been described separately as both an open-air concert and a school dance though the exact details seem somewhat hazy. Either way it was a cornerstone gig for the band. Smith wore motorbike patrolman gear while Taylor dressed in a Harlequin clown suit with top hat. Evans wore red boots and Malcolm dressed in a complete white suit, leaving Angus to wear his schoolboy uniform.

After the successful show, Malcolm felt that the band still needed a stronger overall image, particularly in time for their forthcoming high profile support slots. On May 26, 1974 AC/DC supported Stevie Wright, formally of The Easybeats, at an outdoor concert on the steps of the Sydney Opera House. Wright was promoting his comeback album *Hard Road* and had a big hit with the single 'Evie'. It was an historic concert because it was Sydney's biggest ever outdoor show to date with 25,000 people in attendance. Harry Vanda and George Young both performed in Wright's band, the first time they trio had played together since the 1969 split of the Easybeats. Then in August AC/DC supported Lou Reed after a series of solo club dates of their own. They followed this with their own Can I Sit Next To You Girl Tour.

At the time glam rock was all the rage with UK artists like The Sweet, Slade and David Bowie causing a stir. "I decided to look like the most outrageous rock star," reflected Dave Evans to Mark Prindle of *Citizine* in 2007, "sort of Rod Stewart with his jacket and stuff, that scarf, and also Slade – an English band – wore platform boots, which were pretty new back then. Platform sort of boots and sort of tight pants. So I put both those together and it looked pretty outrageous. We had outrageous outfits."

The gigs that AC/DC performed through 1974 proved to be a great training ground for the band and for Angus to display his seemingly endless bouts of energy. "There's a lot of nonsense spoken about music today," Angus said many years later to Brian Boyd of the UK's *Daily Telegraph* in 2008. "For us it really is quite simple. We began by playing Chuck Berry covers. Every so often we would sneak in one of our own songs. We used to look at each other at the end of our own songs and say, 'I don't think they noticed.' So then we put a few more originals in."

The band's set-lists included many cover versions, notably 'Baby, Please Don't Go', 'Heartbreak Hotel' and various Chuck Berry numbers as well as original songs, 'Can I Sit Next To You, Girl', 'Rockin' In The Parlour', 'Sunset Strip', 'Still In Love', 'Soul Stripper' and 'Rock 'N' Roll Singer'. They also played the odd Free song and even attempted some gutsy Rolling Stones numbers too. They never ventured too far from the blues.

The band's image continued to be a strange mixture of glam and flamboyance which was more British than Aussie; in fact, some Aussie natives thought AC/DC came from England, perhaps London's arty King's Road? However, the glam attire did not naturally match AC/DC's working-class aesthetics and it was ultimately scrapped. Satin and silk just wasn't the sort of look the Young brothers envisaged when they heard the blues. Contrary to popular belief Evans wasn't the only member of AC/DC who looked like a glam rocker – Malcolm also wore silk glam outfits too!

Evans's place was taken sporadically by the band's first manager Dennis Laughlin, which wasn't his first stab at fronting a band: he'd previously been in the Aussie band Sherbet before Daryl Braithwaite joined. At this point AC/DC were playing as many as three gigs per day and so Evans' voice understandably weakened and suffered from over-use (three gigs a day sounds absurd but back then AC/DC would play short sets with mostly cover versions spread throughout the day). It was a sure fire way of building up an audience and reputation as a powerful, fiery live band). Rather than cancel the shows Laughlin stepped in and fronted the band as a quick last minute resort. Evans and Laughlin were not the best of friends and there was some internal tension in the band. Evans later commented to Scott Redeker of *Perris Records* in 2001: "I guess in a nutshell it was about very young musicians with some of us not able to handle egos and jealousies."

"I had actually left the band in Adelaide after a huge argument but stayed on to finish our booking obligations in Perth," Evans reflected during an interview with R. Scott Bolton of *Rough Edge* in 2006. "After arriving back in Melbourne and performing at the last gig of the tour we had a meeting at our hotel and that was when Malcolm said I was no longer in the band. I flew back to Sydney the next day."

What is Dave Evans' legacy as the original singer for AC/DC? Evans had recorded one single with the band: 'Can I Sit Next To You, Girl' with the B-side 'Rockin' In The Parlour' which was finally released in Australia on July 22, 1974. It was a hit Down Under and the Lou Reed tour and the band's own headlining club tour also attracted attention from the Aussie media. 'Can I Sit Next To You, Girl' was never released outside of Australia; it only came out as a 7" single in that country (note the spelling of the title in its original form, as it went on to lose the comma when it was re-recorded with Bon Scott for the later album *High Voltage*).

To promote their first release, AC/DC had performed the song on the popular Aussie TV pop music show *Countdown* earlier in the year but with Neil Smith on bass and drummer Noel Taylor. After Evans' departure from AC/DC, he went on to join the Aussie band Rabbit before enjoying considerable success as a solo artist and eventually residing in Dallas, Texas. He remains a highly respected musician.

AC/DC

The band needed a full-time experienced singer with some rock 'n' roll charisma; somebody with enough charm and verve to take them to the top...

THE ARRIVAL OF BON SCOTT & THE RELEASE OF THE AUSTRALIAN ALBUMS

1974-1975

"AC/DC play basically what was going on with Chuck Berry, Little Richard, Jerry Lee Lewis – trying to create the excitement and get the mood."

Malcolm Young speaking to Tim Henderson of *BW&BK* in 2000

"We knew when we started we wouldn't be accepted overnight; that it was going to be a long haul," Angus confessed to Australia's *Daily Telegraph* journalist Kathy McCabe in 2011. "And our day was different to nowadays; you did every gig in pubs, clubs, whatever show you could get on, whatever tour you could get on and you'd get the odd TV thing, with Ian Meldrum or someone like that. We're not the prettiest bunch of animals in the world. That's a part of it too. But the good thing with us was what people could hear. If people heard it, they felt it."

Indeed, the band knew what they wanted to do right from the get-go and knew how much worked needed to be put into AC/DC for it to be accepted as an authentic rock 'n' roll band.

AC/DC

They also needed some financial backing and a means of marketing their music.

Albert Productions had been formed by businessman Ted Albert back in 1973 and the company would be pivotal for AC/DC to surpass local fame and enjoy international success. Vanda and Young became staff producers for Albert Productions and even roped in the talents of Malcolm and Angus for the Marcus Hook Roll Band project with drummer John Proud and released *Tales Of Old Grand Daddy* in 1973 by EMI. George Young knew that the key to success was playing live and he made his thoughts apparent to AC/DC. George had gone to one of the band's rehearsals and he liked what he heard and he knew there and then that he'd be recording with the band.

AC/DC signed with Albert Productions for Australia and New Zealand which was a major coup at the time for the band as the label's products were distributed by EMI, the legendary London-based record label (the band's line-up would soon be stabilised with the addition of Bon Scott who joined the Young brothers, drummer Phil Rudd and bassist Mark Evans).

"I can't take credit for any of the songs or the success they had once I'd left," AC/DC's original singer Dave Evans graciously reflected to Simon Rushworth of *Rush On Rock* in 2010. "Bon wrote all of those classic songs and I just wouldn't have written them that way. We were very different. But I'm a founding member of the biggest rock and roll band in the world and we had a hit record and it was a wonderful experience while it lasted."

So how did Bon Scott come into the picture, then?

Bon Scott – a friend of George Young – officially joined AC/DC on October 24, 1974. He was born Ronald Belford Scott on July 9, 1946 at the Fyfe Jamieson Maternity Hospital in Forfar, Scotland to Charles Belford and Isabelle Scott. His younger brother Derek was born in 1949 (he had an elder brother named Sandy who died not long after his birth). Ronald Scott was raised in Kirriemuir before moving to Melbourne in Australia aged six in 1952. The Scott family settled in the comfortable Melbourne suburb of Sunshine where Ronald Scott attended the Sunshine Primary School. It was at that school where he got his nickname, Bon. There was already another lad in the class called Ronald so to distinguish him from the other similarly named lad, classmates dubbed the future AC/DC frontman Bon, as in Bonnie Scotland. Bon's second brother was born in 1953. The three Scotts lads had a sister named Valerie.

Bon Scott's first taste of music came in 1956 after the family moved to Fremantle in Western Australia. He became a member of the Fremantle Scots Pipe Band and learned how to play the drums. Afterwards, he dropped out of the John Curtin College Of The Arts aged fifteen and then spent time at a juvenile centre for a number of minor offences. Scott was determined not to repeat these mistakes and took on a number of jobs for a while that included work as a postman, bartender and truck packer before forming his first band The Spektors in 1966 (although conflicting reports suggest it was possibly as early as 1964). He was the band's drummer and sometime singer. It was obvious even back then that Scott had cocky charisma and showmanship which was perfectly suited to rock 'n' roll.

Scott adored Little Richard and set his sights on rock 'n' roll stardom, wanting to follow in the footsteps of his American idol, enjoying both the music of Little Richard but also the rebellious nature of the latter's image. Little Richard was born and raised in Georgia which must have been tough for a young, creative black man in the 1950s. Certainly his upbringing had an impact on his rock 'n' roll persona. Little Richard shocked white America back in the 1950s but the burgeoning teenage generation loved him; he was hugely involved in the seminal birth of rock 'n' roll with a list of now classic and iconic tunes: 'Tutti Frutti', 'Long Tall Sally' and 'Good Golly, Miss Molly'. Jerry Lee Lewis also appealed greatly to Bon Scott, particularly for the alternative attitudes at a very conservative and anti-liberal time in American history. It was not only the birth of shock rock but also punk – they had the image, which was then unique, and the attitude, which was unheard of at the time. Interestingly, many of the rock 'n' roll stars of the 1950s went on to either find or re-embrace God but the impact they made in that decade sent shivers through future generations of music lovers and still resonates to this day. Without them there would be no shock rock or punk rock of any sort. American rock 'n' roll had a major impact on the young Bon Scott.

In late 1996 The Spektors joined forces with another local band named The Winstons and together became known as The Valentines which saw Scott share lead vocals with Vince Lovegrove. The new group had modest success with some original songs, such as 'Every Day I Have To Cry' which was a Top 5 hit. The Valentines split-up due to internal struggles and personal issues after they had a Top 30 hit with 'Juliette', penned by Bon Scott.

The dissolution of The Valentines then prompted Bon Scott to move to Adelaide where he joined the band Fraternity. They released two albums *Livestock* and *Flaming Galah* and then toured in the UK in 1971. It was in the UK when they changed their moniker to Fang and supported Status Quo and Geordie (whose frontman was an amiable and much-liked chap named Brian Johnson, more of him later!). The band toured the UK again a second time and in 1973 went on a long break (they never officially split) which prompted Scott to take a job at the Wallaroo fertiliser plant and it was at this time when he started singing with the Mount Lofty Rangers, a group of musicians led by Peter Head of Headband. Fraternity later reformed with Aussie rock singer Jimmy Barnes replacing Bon Scott. Barnes moved on to other, more high profile ventures, such as a very successful solo career which included a contract with Geffen. He recorded two songs with INXS in 1986: a cover of the Easybeats 'Good Times' and 'Laying Down The Law'. He also recorded a version of 'Simply The Best' with Tina Turner for the Australian League Rugby advertising campaign in 1992. His former band Cold Chisel reformed and released a new album in 2012 called *No Plans*.

Both Fraternity (aka Fang) and Headband shared the same management and after both bands split, the idea of merging musicians from both camps had seemed obvious. The resultant Mount Lofty Rangers, which also included Glen Shorrock, spent time experimenting with songs and it was around this period when Bon Scott, with help from Peter Head, began to compose his own songs and learn about the craft of songwriting. Head also taught Scott how to play the guitar and advised him on how to construct a song which came as a huge joy to the singer after a day at the fertiliser plant. The pair worked well together. Scott sang on Head's 'Round & Round & Round' and 'Carey Gully'. Those rare recordings featuring Bon Scott were heavily bootlegged originally, though Peter Head later deftly added backing arrangements and released very crisp digital versions in 2010. Scott had also composed some original lyrics by himself though he never actually recorded them. The two songs he penned were called 'Bin Up In The Hills Too Long', a witty song showing Bon's tongue-in-cheek style of humour, and 'Clarissa', about a local Adelaide working girl. Scott used to carry around a spiral bound notebook to jot down lyrics and rhymes.

After an altercation between Bon Scott and someone in a bar one night, he jumped on his Suzuki 550 motorbike and rode off. Bon Scott was then involved in a motorbike accident which put him in a three-day coma. He spent a further eighteen days in hospital. Out of hospital, Scott underwent a rehabilitation process aided by his friend Vince Lovegrove and the latter's wife, this included a number of menial jobs. Lovegrove proved to be a great friend and was clearly shocked when he first saw Bon Scott laid up in hospital, as he explained in an article for www.adelaidenow.com.au: 'There was Bon as I had never seen him; limp, smashed to smithereens, his jaw wired, most of his teeth knocked out, a broken collar bone, several cracked and broken ribs, deep cuts across his throat.' Lovegrove openly talks of Bon's 'strong work ethic', despite his wild-man image.

It was during this difficult period that Bon Scott was introduced to AC/DC, then still a glam rock-styled band based in Sydney. Bon Scott came across AC/DC when George Young called the singer telling him the band was on the look out for a new frontman. Malcolm was twenty one and Angus was nineteen. Was Bon too old for AC/DC given that he was born in 1946 when Malcolm was born in 1953 and Angus was born in

AC/DC

1955? And further, did he have the right voice and stage persona? It has been reported that Scott started out as AC/DC's roadie and met up with his old roadie mate, Darcy, from The Valentines. George Young then spoke to his brothers about the possibility of Bon Scott fronting the band, then invited Bon Scott along to a gig at the Pooraka Hotel and met them backstage. Both sides were initially wary of each other due to their age differences but after a jam session back a Bruce Howe's (a friend of Scott's) house it was apparent that Bon Scott and the Youngs had chemistry. They knew how to rock.

Lovegrove had been telling them Scott was perfect for the vacancy; other sources suggest that Gene Pierson was also instrumental in recommending Bon Scott to replace Dave Evans and front AC/DC. Pierson played an integral role in the band's history back then, having previously arranged for programme manager Rod Muir of the rock station 2SM to allow AC/DC to perform on the bill at one of the station's aforementioned school holiday concerts at Chequers.

Bon Scott wanted to be AC/DC's drummer but of course they already had an excellent man on the drum stool (Scott was more experienced as a drummer than a singer and felt more confident on the skins). It was Malcolm who finally got Scott round to the notion of fronting the band. With Scott, what you got is what you saw; he didn't bring an ego with him. When Bon Scott came along it was exactly what AC/DC needed; his age worked *with* the band rather than against it. He stabilised the set-up given their previous tumultuous times and was immediately a strong and positive influence around the young and creatively intense brothers.

Bon Scott's voice would work in the band's favour too; he had a rock side to his vocals but there was also a more melodic, pop side which sprung from his days singing in bands in the 1960s when everyone wanted to be like The Beatles or The Hollies.

It was at this point when AC/DC's career was really launched. The chemistry between their new singer and the Young brothers was obvious right from the start and would prove to be the crux of the band's success later in the decade.

Scott was a warm-hearted and affable bloke who got along with most people although he also kept himself closely guarded; he cherished his privacy. Bon was something of a pop star in Australia because of Fraternity and the success they had Down Under in the early 1970s. 1971's 'Seasons Of Change'/'Summerville' was a hit, 1971's debut album *Livestock* featured Bon on vocals and recorder as does 1972's second album, *Flaming Galah*. Given this and his Scottish background, he got along with the Young's like the proverbial house on fire, despite the age gap.

Scott had clearly put his youthful misdemeanours behind him and turned into a somewhat more rounded individual. Angus spoke to *Sounds* scribe Phil Sutcliffe in 1979 about his own influence on Bon Scott: "I have been a reforming influence. You should have seen the man when I first met him. He couldn't speak English. It was all fuck, cunt, piss, shit. I introduced him to a new side of life. Sent him home with a dictionary."

In the very early days of the band's history, they'd still play a number of cover versions and the set-lists would differ from gig to gig but they also played a healthy number of originals, including but not limited to, 'She's Got Balls', 'High Voltage', 'Soul Stripper', 'Rock 'N' Roll Singer', 'Can I Sit Next To You Girl', 'Little Lover', 'Show Business' and 'Love Song'. Bon Scott and the lads had an immediate onstage rapport with each other and given Bon Scott's background, he knew how to get an audience on his side.

AC/DC were quick to start work on their debut album *High Voltage*, which took just two weeks to get together in November 1974. There were some interesting choices: the catchily-titled 'Soul Stripper' showed off the Young brothers' chemistry; 'Baby, Please Don't Go' is a cover of the Big Joe Williams blues song, originally recorded back in 1935 and covered by Bob Dylan in 1962; 'Little Lover' was originally written by Malcolm when he was fourteen and although the lyrics are not specific it is commonly believed by many that they are about his younger brother's love life. Many of the song's lyrics may appear to be frivolous at first glance but they were certainly introspective for

AC/DC

the time: 'She's Got Balls' was written about Scott's wife Irene (she had been always at his side during his recovery from the motorbike accident and they remained close even after separating).

High Voltage was hastily recorded between gigs at Albert Studios in King Street, Sydney and produced by Harry Vanda and George Young. It was the perfect studio for the band; small, cramped and low-key. There was an energy, aura and vibe there which fuelled Angus's enthusiasm. There were other rooms in the building where Albert Studios was housed but they were too modern and fancy for the Young brothers. They were working-class lads with few expectations beyond making great rock 'n' roll. They recorded everything live in the studio which suited them down to the ground. It gave the band's music a sense of urgency, a vibe and rawness that could not have been more appropriate for AC/DC.

The band recruited session drummer Tony Currenti and also used George Young to lay down some bass parts although on the live front Rob Bailey was playing bass and Peter Clack was playing drums at the time. This has created a confusing chronology within the band's history. In sum, the album's 'total' personnel was made up of Angus Young (lead guitar), Malcolm Young (rhythm guitar, backing vocals, bass guitar and lead guitar), Bon Scott (lead vocals), George Young (bass guitar, rhythm guitar, drums and backing vocals), Rob Bailey (bass guitar), Tony Currenti (drums), Peter Clack (drums) and John Proud (drums).

In the studio, the band were quick to nail down their guitar parts which saw Malcolm play lead on 'Little Lover' and share the lead guitar with Angus on 'Show Business' and 'Soul Stripper'. "I'd just come up with something that fitted the mood of the song," said Angus to Scott Kara of the *New Zealand Herald* in 2010. "A lot of the time I'd be thinking of something very complex but usually, the best thing was the thing that was simple, because it cut right through. So I always thought that was the best approach."

Within ten days, the band had finished recording their debut album. *High Voltage* opens with the blues-soaked chords of 'Baby,

Please Don't Go'. It is not only a tribute to the late great blues legend Big Joe Williams who inspired the likes of the Rolling Stones and ZZ Top, but also a testament to AC/DC's dedication to their blues roots. 'She's Got Balls' is a cheeky number where the band's likable toilet humour comes into play; the chorus is greasy and the vocals raw while the guitars are energetic. 'Little Lover' is a nifty number with a memorable chorus and a noticeable bluesy texture with a taut rhythm section held together by pacey drumming. 'Stick Around' is an average rock track in all honesty but the guitars are suitably gritty and Bon Scott's vocals are full of rock 'n' roll dirt. 'Soul Stripper' sees the tight rhythm section of the band in its early glory with fanatically steady yet heavy drums and Malcolm's relentless bass-line while 'You Ain't Got A Hold On Me' is firmly rooted in 1950s rock 'n' roll where the band's true roots lay and from where they would always draw inspiration. 'Love Song' is a soppy distinctly average affair yet there is something oddly seductive about it, perhaps due in part to the band's obvious passion. 'Show Business' offers little to rave about. The band could have gone out on a much stronger number but they were still learning their craft and better songs would come in time.

High Voltage remains a collector's item amongst AC/DC fans and while it shows promise, the album smacks of fairly basic rock 'n' roll. There is an overall sense of the average, yet there is talent in the songs too and while there are flaws, the Aussie version of *High Voltage* does indeed show promise for bigger and better albums to come.

High Voltage was released on February 17, 1975 in Australia and New Zealand. It peaked at Number 7 in the Australian album charts. This version has never been re-released on any other format anywhere outside of those two countries. The Aussie cover art features an electrical box behind barbed wire while the international release features just a photo of Angus with a yellow electric shock running down the front. The idea for the cover art reportedly came from Albert Productions' Chris Gilbey. Many of the individual tracks were never released outside their adopted homeland of Australia until 1984's *'74 Jailbreak* which includes

AC/DC

'Baby, Please Don't Go', 'You Ain't Got A Hold On Me', 'Soul Stripper' and 'Show Business' while 'Stick Around' and 'Love Song' were included on the 2009 box-set, *Backtracks*. The album's first and only single was 'Love Song (Oh Jene)' which was about Bon Scott's frequent line-up of sexual partners (AC/DC mythology suggests it was meant to be 'Oh Jane' but there was a misprint). Its B-side is the famed 'Baby, Please Don't Go'. The single reached Number 10 in the Australian singles chart.

Reviews of the album were at the time low-key and obviously restricted to Australia and New Zealand. The album went largely unnoticed by critics and sales were modest. It remains a curious album amongst fans and causes some confusion because of the later revamped version for the international market. This Australian version is only remembered by diehard AC/DC fans.

New Year 1975 opened with not only the release of AC/DC's debut album but yet more changes to the band's rhythm section as well as a bunch of club dates around the country. By the time *High Voltage* had been released, the band had upped sticks and moved to Melbourne where they faced some major line-up changes. Drummer Peter Clack had departed in January to be replaced permanently by Phil Rudd the following month. Clack had appeared in the first piece of video footage available of AC/DC: *The Last Picture Show Theatre* video of the band's first ever single, 'Can I Sit Next To You, Girl', so his part in AC/DC's history is assured!

Phil Rudd was exactly the kind of drummer AC/DC needed for their hard rock, energetic style. Born Phillip Hugh Norman Witschke Rudzevecuis on May 19, 1954 in Melbourne, Rudd was an experienced drummer by the time he joined AC/DC. He'd been in a number of bands in his home city and even played in Buster Brown with future Rose Tattoo frontman Angry Anderson. Buster Brown released just one album: 1974's *Something To Say*. After Buster Brown, Rudd joined Coloured Balls but his tenure didn't last long before he heard from Trevor Young of Coloured Balls that AC/DC were auditioning for a new drummer. Rudd's hard rhythmic stomp was perfect for

During the filming of 'Jailbreak' in 1975.
Courtesy of Philip Morris/Rex Features

AC/DC

AC/DC and he was hired on the spot. One of Rudd's primary influences growing up was Free and Bad Company drummer Simon Kirke whose drumming technique is never anything less than masterful.

Bassist Rob Bailey, who'd also played on the Dave Evans sung 'Can I Sit Next To You, Girl' and appeared in the aforementioned video also departed in January and ironically, was replaced by former AC/DC bassist Larry Van Kriedt who joined the band for just a few days although it wouldn't be until March that a more permanent replacement was found in Mark Evans. During the lull, Malcolm and George Young played the role of bassist as did Phil Matters and Bruce Howe, temporarily. Evidently it didn't work out with those guys so when Evans was hired the band was pleased to finally have a seemingly permanent bass player.

Mark Evans was born Mark Whitmore Evans on March 2, 1956 in Melbourne. He became interested in rock 'n' roll as a teenager when he discovered the likes of Jerry Lee Lewis, Chuck Berry and Elvis Presley. He was originally interested in Aussie Rules football but the lure of music forced him to pick up a bass which he swapped for a guitar before going back to bass again. When he started to play the bass on a more serious level he became interested in bands like Cream, Black Sabbath, Deep Purple and Led Zeppelin. He was also a fan of English glam rock bands such as The Sweet and Slade.

Evans had grown up with AC/DC's roadie Steve McGrath as childhood friends with the pair being fervent football pals. One day in March 1975 they met up to play pool together and watch a live band at the Station Hotel in Melbourne, which had gained a strong name for itself on account of all the bands that had used it as a springboard to get on the live circuit. McGrath told Evans that AC/DC, the band which he was working for, were looking for a bass player and that an audition was being held soon. Evans was so keen on the idea he hung around to see AC/DC live that very afternoon and met them after the gig.

"What got my attention was two of the guys in the band, their elder brother is George Young from The Easybeats," Evans told the author during an interview for the rock website *Rocktopia* in

2012. "I was and always will be an Easybeats fan. I just love the band. That got my attention and I just went around and met them and got a copy of the record [*High Voltage*] and went back and played it the next day. Two days later I was back with them at the Station Hotel. It all happened very quickly…"

AC/DC now had a bass player which gave Malcolm the chance to rush back to rhythm guitar. "It's interesting because I mostly saw Malcolm play bass with the band at the gig at the Station Hotel," Evans told the author in said interview. "What actually happened is: I went and saw the band; they played the first set as a four-piece and then I played the second set with 'em which was a major part of the *High Voltage* album. I watched Malcolm play bass and I've gotta tell you he is a knockout bass player, man. I don't think people realise how deeply versed he is in guitar playing. Malcolm is very good at selecting and sticking at what's right for the band. He's one hell of a guitar player. He could knock out all that jazz stuff like you wouldn't believe."

He continued: "The style of bass playing that has become known as the AC/DC style of bass playing was very different from Malcolm's style. I always thought Malcolm's style of playing was influenced by Andy Fraser. The most perfect bass player for that band Free you can ever imagine. Malcolm was very 'notey'… a lot like George was with his bass playing. On the early albums you hear George play on some of the stuff. I played on some of the stuff. George played bass on the single 'High Voltage' because that was recorded before I joined the band. It was very loopy, almost Ronnie Lane [of Small Faces] sort of bass playing. It didn't influence me but I think that once the rhythm guitar was back in there that's AC/DC completely. Malcolm gave me a lot more latitude and I don't think he could get back on that rhythm guitar fast enough."

Evans was nineteen when he joined the band and was working as a daytime clerk at the pay section of the Postmaster-General's Department. Naturally joining AC/DC would prove to be quite a career change for the newly acquired bassist. Evans hastily learned all the songs from *High Voltage* after he'd gotten a copy and he only met Bon Scott on the day of his first performance with the band on the TV show *Countdown* where they played 'Baby, Please Don't Go' with Bon Scott famously dressed as a school girl.

"It was obvious to me that he would split from the band and go off and do his own thing quite a bit," Evans said about Bon Scott to the author for an interview in *Rocktopia* in 2012. "He liked his own space. There was quite a marked age difference between us; I was the youngest and Bon was the oldest. When you're nineteen and someone's twenty nine, that's a massive difference. It's like having your old man on the road with you [laughs]. Great guy, man, I've gotta tell you. I suppose when I first met him it would have been absolutely impossible for Bon not to be welcoming. He was just a really warm guy. He was generous and there was just a lovely way about him."

The *Countdown* performance was used as the official video for the band's first single with Scott, as a B-side to 'Love Song (Oh Jene)' from the *High Voltage* sessions ('Love Song (Oh Jene)' does not actually appear on the album; it is a very rare collectors' item and is highly sought after by fans). After only a few days in the band Mark Evans was already appearing on national television.

AC/DC included the iconic blues number 'Baby, Please Don't Go' in their live sets, which would be a fan favourite despite it not being an original AC/DC song. AC/DC's version of the song has become something of a cult classic. The Aussie rock radio stations played 'Baby, Please Don't Go' rather than the A-side 'Love Song (Oh Jene)'. Indeed had they chosen to play the A-side instead and ignored 'Baby, Please Don't Go' than maybe AC/DC might not have broken the way they did? The future could have been quite different otherwise.

Some bands have fairly consistent line-ups during the first few years before everything changes. Queen springs to mind; surely they had one of the most consistent line-ups in rock history? Van Halen and Black Sabbath had consistent line-ups in the early years before that too changed. However, AC/DC's line-up history prior to Bon Scott's arrival and even immediately thereafter is confusing with some members lasting only weeks. In spring 1975, AC/DC would enter a seemingly permanent line-up that would last for the foreseeable future: singer Bon Scott, lead guitarist Angus Young, rhythm guitarist Malcolm Young, drummer Phil Rudd and bassist Mark Evans.

"If you ask me very plainly whose band it was, it was Malcolm's band," opined Mark Evans to John Parks of *Legendary Rock Interviews* in 2011. "That was made very clear to me at the start and it was implicit that it was Malcolm's band during my era. It was George running the record company and producing and, yeah, it could make it difficult at times for the rest of us but to be honest the positive output of those brothers all working together far outweighed anything negative."

The band had already begun promoting the album with a tour of Australia that commenced on February 24, 1975 at Chequers in Sydney and ended at the International Hotel in Melbourne in September. However, the *High Voltage* Tour was hit by a problem when drummer Phil Rudd injured his hand and ironically the band re-hired drummer Colin Burgess to temporarily replace the injured Rudd during September.

As soon as Rudd was fit enough to rejoin the band it was obvious that there was a chemistry between himself and Mark Evans. "For the life of me I can't understand why he is so [underrated]," Evans commented during an interview with the author in 2010 for *Rocktopia*. "If you ask guys who are good rock 'n' roll drummers that I've paired up with over the years like Simon [Wright] who was playing with AC/DC for a while [they'd say] there are guys that should be mentioned in the same group like Simon Kirke, Charlie Watts and Phil. I know Simon Kirke was a massive influence on Phil. He is highly underrated. I know he is the best drummer I've ever played with. I know he's important because the times I've seen the band when Phil wasn't with them – with all respect to [future AC/DC drummers] Simon [Wright] and Chris [Slade] – it's a very different band from when Phil wasn't there. It was always great but it's like taking Charlie Watts out of the Stones. The part would be missing without Charlie and I think it's the same with Phil."

The band worked very quickly on their second Australia-released only album, *T.N.T.*; like its predecessor, *T.N.T.* was crafted in just two weeks. The backing tracks were done in the first week while throughout the second week they laid down the lead vocals, guitars, bass and drums before George and Vanda mixed the album. The band used all the material they had at that point so there are no leftover tracks from the *T.N.T.* sessions. All the instruments would be plugged in and miked up and there'd be Phil Rudd in one room of the two-room studio and the Young brothers in the other room.

Ironically, one such track named 'High Voltage' does not appear on the original Australian release. The nine-track album includes seven songs that were penned by the Young brothers with Bon Scott as well as the catchy 'Can I Sit Next To You Girl' which was written by Malcolm and Angus. AC/DC fans in Australia were already familiar with 'Can I Sit Next To You, Girl' which had been written and recorded when Dave Evans was fronting the band; however, the new version with Scott singing was a minute longer and with amended lyrics and slightly different arrangements. Also, the Bon Scott version omits the comma before 'Girl' in the title thus distinguishing it from the Dave Evans recording. The re-recorded version ('Can I Sit Next To You Girl') features singer Bon Scott, the Young brothers on guitars, bassist Mark Evans and drummer Phil Rudd. Bon Scott was a fan of T-Rex's Marc Bolan who was a source of inspiration for 'Can I Sit Next To You Girl.' The band also stayed close to their blues roots by covering the 1957 Chuck Berry song 'School Days'.

T.N.T. was recorded at Albert Studios in Sydney during July of 1975 and produced by Harry Vanda and George Young. It was recorded live as a band; that's the way they worked best. Angus had enough cigarettes while Bon had Stone's Green Ginger Wine aplenty and this fuelled the album's tempo and aggression. The band had developed what would become their trademark sound by ditching the glam rock element and adopting a harder, more focussed R&B sound akin to their influences. It was obvious that the band craved to develop a sound that was not too dissimilar from the English bands that came out of the South of England in the 1960s, including The Kinks, Cream and The

Yardbirds. This sound can be heard in tracks like 'Rocker', 'The Jack', 'It's A Long Way To The Top (If You Wanna Rock 'N' Roll)' and 'High Voltage'. With Mark Evans on bass and Phil Rudd on drums, it represented the band's first album with a seemingly steady line-up.

It was the first time Mark Evans – an eager young bassist from Melbourne – had ever set foot in a studio. Fortunately, George Young was more than helpful and mentored Evans through the entire recording process. The three Young brothers were a very strong trio; they trusted each other implicitly.

It was a whirlwind time for Mark Evans as newest member of the band. He was even told straight away by a member of the band's team Rob The Roadie that the band would be moving to the UK at some point in the next couple of years which gave Evans a lot to think about. Most of his favourite bands came from the UK so he was looking forward to getting into the English rock scene. AC/DC really came into its own with Bon Scott and certainly Phil Rudd brought a hell of a lot to the band's rhythm sound too with his deep and steady drumming. Mark Evans cemented the stable line-up.

Mark Evans spoke to the author for an interview on the rock website *Rocktopia* in 2012: "What seemed to happen in Malcolm and Angus's situation was they had a blueprint from when they were kids; from when they were in primary school. They watched what happened with George when George was in The Easybeats. They were massive in England. They had a Top 5 hit in the States. They looked like at one stage they could have been the next Kinks. What's a better rock-pop song than 'Friday On My Mind'? It was completely normal for them to envision being in a successful and international rock band. The idea was not alien to them. There wasn't so much desperation as an expectation. I'm sure they couldn't guarantee that it was goin' to happen but they had a pretty good idea how it all worked and where it was going to go. Having George involved and Albert Productions was certainly the easy way through but the talent was there too. It's obvious to me that the band really did start when Bon joined. Previous to Bon joining there was a whole bunch of line-ups.

AC/DC

I tried to count the bass players before me and I think it's something like eight and that was in a twelve-month period. It happened quickly and they had about three or four drummers and there was another singer. The band's timeline starts in October 1974 when Bon joined the band. They were in the studio the month after that working on their first album so it happened very quickly."

However, Rudd and Evans had very little input and even Bon Scott didn't have a lot of influence because everything was governed by Malcolm, Angus and George Young. Sure, there'd be disagreements between the three brothers and sometimes they'd get pretty heated but it was all for the good of the band. This begs the question: were the rest of the band members merely hired guns? Well, no! Rudd, Evans and certainly the now iconic Scott brought their own traits to the band, albeit those contributions were subtle at first.

In the studio it was George's idea to include the bagpipes on 'It's A Long Way To The Top (If You Wanna Rock 'N' Roll)' which derived from an extended jam session that was started by Malcolm. George thought Bon Scott played bagpipes in a previous band when he was actually the drummer but Scott picked up the pipes and learned how to play the instrument quickly and even went on to play them onstage. It kept him close to his Scottish roots, which he was forever proud of. Another classic on the album is 'The Jack' which was about venereal disease. Bon Scott told *Sounds* writer Phil Sutcliffe in 1976: "We were living with this houseful of ladies who were all very friendly and everyone in the band had got the jack. So we wrote this song and the first time we did it on stage they were all in the front row with no idea what was goin' to happen."

Bon sang the repetitive chorus line and pointed at certain women in the front row but word got around and at future shows the female members of the audience went to the back of the clubs when 'The Jack' was performed!

The initial lyrics that Scott penned were said to be very explicit, too graphic for the radio so they were toned down for commercial reasons. Bon Scott had something of a reputation when it came to his sexual conquests and some of the band's lyrics surely referred to his experiences with women.

Interestingly, another moment of inspiration from George Young came when he heard Angus singing "oi" to himself and suggested they add it to the title track which has since become a classic and a live favourite. 'T.N.T.' came out of a songwriting session the three Young brothers had around a piano.

"I can always remember Angus walking around reciting the words to 'T.N.T.'" commented Evans during an interview with the author for the rock website *Rocktopia* in 2012. "That's one of the things I will point to, also; Angus and Malcolm have a history of writing a lot of lyrics right back to 'Can I Sit Next To You, Girl' and 'Rock 'N' Roll Singer'. It's completely natural; they're used to coming up with a lot of ideas."

T.N.T. opens with the indestructible force of 'It's A Long Way To The Top (If You Wanna Rock 'N' Roll)' before the catchy 'Rock 'N' Roll Singer' shows off some nifty guitar work. The now classic song 'The Jack' is an absolute blast right the way through and 'Live Wire' is perhaps the album's heaviest song. 'T.N.T.' is one of the band's most anthemic rock songs and is now hailed as a classic. 'Rocker' is still one of the band's fastest songs and a testament to their love of the likes of Little Richard and Jerry Lee Lewis; simple but effective. 'Can I Sit Next To You Girl' is a bluesy understated affair while 'High Voltage' is a basic but wholly entertaining salute to rock 'n' roll. The album closes with 'School Days', a cover of the Chuck Berry song which the band had played regularly at their shows.

Even at this stage AC/DC had already begun to strengthen and refine their sound and while there were still teething problems they knew about the elements of the basic formula for a memorable rock song. The guitars craved some more work and the chorus needed to be strengthened but they showed promise and *T.N.T.* was a giant leap forward from *High Voltage*; released earlier in the year. *T.N.T.* proved that there were two sides to the band, merging their primary influences together to create what would become the electrifying AC/DC sound. There was the blues sound not just of Southern America with black artists like

AC/DC

Muddy Waters, Robert Johnson and B.B. King but also the white hard rock blues of 1960s Britain; The Yardbirds, Led Zeppelin and Cream, amongst others. AC/DC combined that sound with the rock 'n' roll of 1950s America; Elvis, Eddie Cochran and of course, Angus's hero Chuck Berry and Bon Scott's idol, Little Richard.

T.N.T. still sounds like a young band trying to find their voice and their sound but there are some gems on the album that have stood the test of time; 'It's A Long Way To The Top (If You Wanna Rock 'N' Roll)' is the perfect example. There is an obvious rawness throughout the album but also an endless run of energy typical of a young and thirsty working-class rock 'n' roll band. They wisely chose to remake 'Can I Sit Next To You Girl' while the rebellious nature of the album with songs like 'The Jack' and 'Rocker' would help the album age remarkably well. Similar to the band's very first album *High Voltage*, *T.N.T.* is a collector's item amongst AC/DC zealots because of its limited release and is little heard of these days with most fans favouring the international version of *High Voltage*. Confused? Then read on…

T.N.T. was released in Australia and New Zealand in December, 1975 and spawned the singles 'High Voltage' (released back in July) and 'It's A Long Way To The Top (If You Wanna Rock 'N' Roll)'. Both songs would become AC/DC classics and hard rock anthems for generations to come. *T.N.T.* hit Number 1 in the Aussie Kent Music Report Album Charts, which was the country's then-national album charts compiled by David Kent (before the Australian Recording Industry Association was founded in the 1980s and compiled the country's national charts). In New Zealand, the album hit Number 35.

T.N.T. was released in a wonderfully packaged gatefold sleeve LP with fake police ID cards containing the personal details of the band members such as date of birth although Angus Young's was listed as 1959 rather than the correct year of 1955 which meant he was sixteen rather than twenty; as mentioned, it helped his schoolboy image seem more authentic.

Causing much confusion amongst fans, the original version of *T.N.T.* includes longer versions of 'Can I Sit Next To You Girl' and 'High Voltage' than those featured on the CD reissues and the international version of *High Voltage* while the same can be said for 'Rocker', which was included on the band's second international release, *Dirty Deeds Done Dirt Cheap*.

T.N.T. like its predecessor *High Voltage* has never been re-released by any other label outside of Australia and New Zealand. *T.N.T.* spawned three singles: the title track (with the B-side 'Rocker') was released and hit Number 11 Down Under back in March; 'High Voltage' was released in July before the band began recording *T.N.T.* and given the title many fans naturally assumed it was from their debut album; it peaked at Number 6 in the Australian charts. 'High Voltage' was eventually released in the UK as a single in 1980 and reached Number 48; it had also had a European release back in 1976. In Australia, the B-side was 'Soul Stripper' while in the UK and Europe it was 'Live Wire'.

The album's title track has become one of the band's most memorable songs especially onstage where they have gotten the audience to sing along to the chorus. Finally, 'It's A Long Way To The Top (If You Wanna Rock 'N' Roll)' was released in December (with the B-side 'Can I Sit Next To You Girl') of the same year and peaked at Number 5 in Australia.

Reviews of the album were, like its predecessor, minimal and largely Australian-based for obvious reasons. A lot of critics did not get the band's sense of humour and nor did they seem to understand the point of the group. What did AC/DC have to offer? Some critics simply found AC/DC to be obnoxious and annoying but those very critics didn't understand that AC/DC was exactly what Australia needed and nor did any of the naysayers realise just how important AC/DC would be to the country and even to the Australian economy in the future.

T.N.T.'s legacy at the time was largely restricted to the most enthusiastic of AC/DC fans because its release was limited to the band's native country and nearby New Zealand. Much of the album went on to form the international version of *High Voltage* which was the band's first worldwide album.

Like many AC/DC albums, *T.N.T.* has grown in stature over the years with many critics revising their initial opinions while younger critics have praised certain aspects of the album so it is worthwhile knowing what contemporary reviewers think.

Writing on the popular reference website *All Music Guide*, Eduardo Rivadavia said in his positive review of the album: "*T.N.T.*, though largely lost to ancient history, was a stellar album in its own right, and especially crucial in that it marked AC/DC's definitive break with their now seemingly heretical glam rock inclinations, in order to embrace the blue collar hard rock hat would forever after be their trademark."

To promote the album the band launched the *T.N.T.* Australian Tour, which lasted a few months at the tail-end of 1975. The band did struggle to find success; it certainly didn't come rushing to them. Sometimes they'd only be playing to thirty people at a show but those thirty people would tell their friends and the next gig would have 35 people and so the audiences grew and grew. There wasn't a lot of money in those days and any cash they did make went back into the band. They spent so much time on the road that they didn't have time to buy anything. They certainly didn't have any money; nothing to splash out on expensive equipment or instruments. There was only a spare guitar between the Young brothers. That's just the humble way they lived.

They had to believe in themselves to make it big and they certainly felt that they had something special to give to the world. Sure, the band liked to party and meet girls but the music came first. *Always*. Angus never drank and Evans didn't even smoke cigarettes but others did enjoy beer and a whiskey! Playing onstage really helped the band in the studio; it sharpened them, made them more confident. Angus smoked like a chimney and given his intense working regime it was like adding fuel to the fuel. Both Angus and Malcolm are very driven, hard-working individuals. No one could find Angus's switch-off button.

Was touring becoming too much? Bon Scott certainly had his demons but he never missed a show. There were times when he'd disappear on his own and some of the band's crew wondered if he'd make the show on time, but he always did. Scott wasn't the only member of the band to show up five minutes before they were due to go onstage. It was part and parcel of the band's crazy

Bon Scott onstage in 1976.
Courtesy of Chris Capstick/Rex Features

lifestyle back in those hectic early days. During one show, Malcolm and Scott had to play the drums and bass to kick off a gig because the other members had not yet turned up. Audiences began to think it was part of the AC/DC live experience.

What was the state of Australian rock at this time? Where did AC/DC fit into the Aussie rock scene? The scene Down Under is said to have gone through various periods of change during the 1960s and 1970s. Certainly the first bands to have had success outside of Australia were the mid-1960s acts The Easybeats and English-born brothers, the Bee Gees. These guys were influenced by the British Invasion bands like The Beatles and The Hollies but before them there was also the Sydney-born singer Johnny O'Keefe whose hits included 'Wild One' and 'She's My Baby'. Like the Young brothers of AC/DC, the aforementioned Aussie artists were also influenced by the American rockabilly stars such as Eddie Cochran, Elvis Presley and Little Richard. Another big Australian singer of the day was the Manchester-born guitarist, singer-songwriter Billy Thorpe of Billy Thorpe & The Aztecs whose hits included 'Poison Ivy', 'Sick And Tired' and 'Over The Rainbow'.

During the mid-to-late 1960s, there weren't just The Easybeats and the Bee Gees but a whole movement of Australia-based bands inspired by American rock 'n' roll and the British Invasion bands, including but certainly not limited to: Masters Apprentices, Ray Brown & the Whispers, the Loved Ones, Lyne Randell, the Twilights and Max Merritt. Other Australia acts started to emerge in the early 1970s, which is known as the Third Wave, and those artists were the likes of The Flying Circus, Steve Wright, Blackfeather and Russell Morris *et al*. However, fewer and fewer Australian bands were making a splash outside of their native country.

The Aussie pop TV show *Countdown* was launched in late 1974 and provided a major platform for young native bands and certainly helped them gain notice outside of the country. AC/DC had little, if anything, in common with a lot of Aussie bands that came before them. A major change came in the mid-1970s and that was with the birth and rise of pub rock championed by bands such as Cold Chisel, Dragon, Australian Crawl, The Sports, The Angels, Richard Clapton and a band that became AC/DC's only serious native competitors, Rose Tattoo who formed in 1976 and released their first single 'Bad Boy For Love', from their self-titled debut album, in 1977.

With two albums under their belt, both of which were released in less than twelve months, 1975 was an intense year for AC/DC; their popularity was growing all over Australia, which was largely due to their intensive live performances and constant touring. They also appeared on TV and radio was beginning to support them more. However, the band's first two albums had only been released in Australia and New Zealand so for them to make it big abroad they had to move to either the UK or the USA. Could they make the breakthrough to the next level?

HIGH VOLTAGE &
DIRTY DEEDS DONE
DIRT CHEAP
1976

"Blues is a big part of rock and roll. The best rock and roll got its birth in the blues. You hear it in Little Richard and Chuck Berry."
Angus Young speaking to Alan Di Perna
of *Guitar World* in 2000

1976 would turn out to be the most important year for AC/DC up to that point in their history. They began the year touring, first with the renowned *Lock Up Your Daughters* Summer Vacation Tour of Australia in January followed by an extensive set of sweat-induced club dates. The name of the tour derives from a line in the now iconic song 'T.N.T.'.

On February 23, the band filmed the first of three official promotional music videos for the single 'It's A Long Way To The Top (If You Wanna 'N' Roll)' on the back of a truck driving down Swantson Street in Melbourne with members of The Rats Of Tobruk Pipe Band. As a testament to the band's growing legacy and impact on Aussie culture, Corporation Lane in Melbourne (which features in the video to 'It's A Long Way To The Top

AC/DC

(If You Wanna Rock 'N' Roll)') was renamed AC/DC Lane on October 1, 2004 in tribute to the band.

"I think the most exhilarating moment I shared with the guys was when we were in northern New South Wales on the *Lock Up Your Daughters* Tour," Mark Evans recalled to Rob Cavuoto of *Guitar International* in 2011. "We were listening to the local radio station and 'Long Way To The Top' came on with that big guitar intro and we said, 'Fuck! What a bad sound. It's fucking fantastic!' For it to jump out of the radio completely unannounced, everyone looked around the car and went, 'Man, this is happening.' To have a common moment with the guys, the five of us, sitting in the car listening to that was absolutely exhilarating."

They later performed 'T.N.T.' on the Australian TV music show *Countdown* as the album had given the band a lot of exposure Down Under. AC/DC then commenced the *High Voltage* Tour of Europe which began at the Red Cow in Hammersmith, London on April 23. The story goes that the band were only playing to about fifty people at the start of their first London gig but by the end of the first set because of the sheer noise and word of mouth the audience had hugely increased inside the venue. AC/DC were making their mark in England. The first AC/DC UK tour officially commenced on May 11 after several low-key UK dates, with the band headlining their first gig at the famed London venue, The Marquee, on June 4.

"I can't comment directly for them what it was like but I can tell you directly what it looked like to me: it looked fantastic," Mark Evans said to the author for the rock website *Rocktopia* in 2012, when asked what it was like travelling around the UK and seeing the Young brothers and Bon Scott reconnecting with their native Scotland. "They were having a ball. With Angus and Malcolm they can be at times a little guarded but I've gotta tell you when we stopped off at Stirling Castle [in Glasgow] it was just great. They were into it, man. It meant a lot to them. We did at gig in Glasgow ... and there were signs from people saying, 'WELCOME HOME'. Those boys are Scots. Seeing them reconnect with Scotland was a joy, let me tell you."

Although Bon Scott was much calmer than in his less law-abiding younger years, he was still known for enjoying the rock 'n' roll lifestyle. It was his character, in his blood to live the life he wanted to live and not necessarily follow the rules. Certainly the nine to five, Monday to Friday lifestyle was never going to be suitable for him. "He's wilder than any of us," Malcolm told revered *Sounds* scribe Phil Sutcliffe in 1976 after the band had just moved to London where they rented a flat and filled it with secondhand furniture and a colour TV. "One time in New Zealand he was really plastered standing eight foot up on a stack of amps singing when he got hit on the head by a full beer can. He thought he saw who did it and he jumped straight off the amps then off the stage into the crowd and he was piling into these four Maoris when the bouncers got there."

The band moved around Europe thereafter giving the UK a break from the sheer intensity of an AC/DC tour. However, they did return to the UK to play a residency at The Marquee from July 26 to August 23 much to the delight of the Young brothers who craved success in the English capital. However, such was the zealous nature of the band's growing fanbase that the ticket allocation of just seven hundred was far exceeded by the hardcore rockers lined up outside attempting to gatecrash the venue. They also managed to get a slot on the iconic Reading Festival on August 29 and so it seemed that AC/DC's plan of worldwide rock 'n' roll domination was coming into play.

"Loved it!" Evans exclaims when asked by the author for the rock website *Rocktopia* in 2012 about his experiences travelling around the UK and Europe. "Ever since I was little I've not been intrigued by the travelling *per se* but I was intrigued by other countries and how countries can be so different from what I was used to in Melbourne. I was also intrigued by the Pyramids or Big Ben or the Eiffel Tower. It would be great to see those sorts of things. It's something I always wanted to do. [Touring] was a great way to do it. We spent time in Europe and it was great. I'm from a generation of Anglo-Australians – I'm an Aussie – where there are ties to Britain so to get there was just a blast. I love London. We went to places like Manchester and Liverpool."

AC/DC

Enjoying a rare break during a hectic decade! L-R: Malcolm Young, Mark Evans, Bon Scott, Angus Young, Phil Rudd.
Courtesy of News Ltd/Newspix/Rex Features

The iconic guitarist Ritchie Blackmore, however, seemed rather dismissive of AC/DC: "I like them as friends but I don't like their music," he later told *3DB Radio* in Melbourne on November 21, 1976.

AC/DC had left Australia and made London their home while they concentrated on finding success abroad and it seemed to be working in their favour. The band had signed an international deal with Atlantic and released their debut *High Voltage* to rock fans outside of Australia and New Zealand. The London-based label thought it would be best to release a compilation of the first two albums as the band were about to move to the UK and attempt to make a dent in the potentially lucrative UK/Europe market. The international version of *High Voltage* would act as a sort of introduction to AC/DC. The UK had already been treated to the band's live performances just a few short weeks previously so it was time for them to get their hands on an AC/DC album.

The amalgamated European release of *High Voltage* begins with 'It's A Long Way To The Top (If You Wanna Rock 'N' Roll)', almost the perfect AC/DC song, with bagpipes thrown in too! The descending guitars show some perfect interplay between Malcolm and Angus and Bon's voice is suitably charged, presumably perhaps with whiskey. 'Rock 'N' Roll Singer' is another one of the band's homages to the genre they love so passionately and a testament to their dedication to rock 'n' roll. There's some catchy lead work from Angus and some perfectly steady drums. The toilet humour of 'The Jack' shows the band at their funniest whilst the slightly jazz tinge to the drums and the bluesy guitars recalls some of the band's influences. Given the lyrics and Bon's vocal performance it's easy to see why this song helped the band build up a rapport with their audiences at gigs. 'Live Wire' is a deceptively heavy song; the sturdy drums, deep bass and steady guitars give the song a powerful stomp but Bon steals the show on this one although the guitar solo is quite nifty. 'T.N.T.' needs little examination; despite the relatively simple lyrics this song is one of the band's most enjoyable tracks from any AC/DC album. The plain but effective riff, the steady melody and memorable lyrics make this an almost perfect live rock song. Indeed, it would become a permanent fixture in the band's future set-lists for this reason. 'Can I Sit Next To You Girl' sees Mark Evans turn out a strong bass-line that helps propel the track while the bluesy guitar work of Angus shows that the band hadn't lost touch with their 1950s rock 'n' roll influences. Given the lyrical nature of the song and Bon's manly vocals, there's something atmospheric about this track but the toe-tapping melody makes it a guilty pleasure of sorts. Meanwhile, 'Little Lover' slows down the tempo to a mid-paced bluesy vibe while 'She's Got Balls' is a hoot. The album closes with the electric shocks of 'High Voltage', a thrilling song with a terrific little riff. What better way to close the album?

Overall, *High Voltage* contains some flaws such as the ordinary production and it lacks the meaty guitars that would later become the band's trademark, but it's still not without a dose of classic tracks.

The international release of *High Voltage* came on May 14, 1976. It peaked at Number 7 in France and eventually hit Number 146 in the USA. Just to confuse fans even more, the international versions of the album had different covers: the European release looked slightly glam with lots of multi-colouring but another version featured the same cover as the single for 'It's A Long Way To The Top (If You Wanna Rock 'N' Roll)' while the running time for both this song and 'High Voltage' differ from the original Australian releases.

The press treated *High Voltage* somewhat harshly especially in the USA after it was released over there on September 28. Billy Altman, writing in *Rolling Stone* on December 16, said the band and the album were an "all-time low" for rock 'n' roll. Harsh words for sure. Perhaps the band were stung by Altman's review a little bit but they didn't show it. Even the heaviest hearted rockers get a little upset by bad reviews especially from important publications with wide readerships. However, the band took it with a good dose of humour which is their way. AC/DC were punk before punk came along; they had the objectionable volume, the aggression, attitude and cheeky humour. They forgot about the bad reviews and moved on. Well, the album did go on to sell three million copies worldwide.

Other later reviews of the album have been far more favourable than the original batch of reviews back in 1976. Gret Kot wrote in *Rolling Stone* during the time of the AC/DC reissues in 2003: "AC/DC showed how much fun true tastelessness could be and how liberating it could sound. These Australian delinquents played their bloodshot blues rock with the venom of punk rockers and the swagger of drunken lechers."

"There are songs about rock 'n' roll," wrote Stephen Thomas Erlewine on *All Music Guide*, "slow sleazy blues, high-voltage boogie, double entendres so obvious they qualify as single entendres and, of course, the monster riffs of Angus Young, so big and bold they bruise the listener upon contact. It's those riffs – so catchy they sound lifted when they're original, so simple they're often wrongly dismissed as easy – that give the music its backbone, the foundation for Bon Scott to get dirty, and rockers never got quite as dirty as Bon Scott."

High Voltage certainly set the tone for future albums and while it may not count as one of their finest efforts, there's no question that it contains some of the band's most memorable tunes. It's a modest Bon Scott effort but significantly better than the band's weaker albums of the 1980s.

AC/DC had moved over to the UK and by this point in 1976, the punk movement had rooted itself firmly into the minds and consciousness of the British public especially with a generation of disillusioned youths. It was more that just a music trend; it was sub-cultural movement that changed the ideology of a generation of youths, mostly male. It was located primarily in the inner streets of London and New York. Unlike some bands that rely heavily on long guitar riffs and progressive chord structures such as ELP, AC/DC survived the punk era with gusto. AC/DC were one of those rare bands that appealed to punk audiences as well as hard rock fans, largely because of their lack of pretentiousness and their raw and electrifying sound. Most of the UK's music press treated AC/DC as a punk band with the exception of *Sounds*, which championed the traditional UK rock scene. Even Led Zeppelin looked old in comparison to these disgruntled punk rockers. There was also some rebelliousness about AC/DC (like Angus mooning at audiences) that punk fans found entertaining.

There were a few other bands that survived the punk era rather well such as Queen who released the masterful hard rock album *News Of The World* during the zenith of the controversial punk era. Heavy metal band Judas Priest also ploughed through the era with hands-fisted-and-in-the-air gusto. Even to this day, forty years after the inception of the band, AC/DC continue to follow their own rules and it serves them well. They have often given the middle finger sign to anyone that has even attempted to change their ethos.

AC/DC had spent the previous three years building up a fanbase in Australia and playing obscure small towns that a lot of bands wouldn't or couldn't visit and so when they moved to the UK they started from scratch. Although they had already played blistering music at The Marquee, that was a small venue and very much 'a London thing'; the wider provinces of the UK were still virgin territory to the band. By playing much smaller, more provincial towns they wanted to win over the rest of Britain. Some of the best places to play in the UK have always been working-class towns and cities in the North of England such as Sheffield and Newcastle or Glasgow in Scotland. They are rock lovin' areas and AC/DC went down like the proverbial storm. Sometimes they'd play as many as six or seven gigs a week on both sides of Hadrian's Wall.

Everything AC/DC did they did with humour; how on earth could they take themselves seriously when their guitarist – a grown man – is dressed as a schoolboy? Comedy was an essential part of the band's ethos in life and music. The humour was especially evident during the Bon Scott years.

They were due to tour the UK hitting various clubs and small venues with the blues rock band Back Street Crawler beginning April 25, but because of the sudden and tragic death of ex-Free guitarist Paul Kossoff on March 19 from a heart attack during

AC/DC

a Los Angeles to New York overnight flight, AC/DC ended up with three weeks off before touring resumed. It was possibly the longest time the band had off from touring at that point.

This was still an intense period for the band because in just two weeks they recorded much of their next album, *Dirty Deeds Done Dirt Cheap*. 'Rocker' had been culled from *T.N.T.* while the band used original songs to make up the rest of the album. The songs were all written by Malcolm and Angus Young and Bon Scott and made overzealous use of double entendres which had become one of their trademarks; take 'Big Balls' for example. They recorded a song called 'I'm A Rebel' in September 1976 with their elder brother Alex Young on lead vocals and Bon Scott – who was said to be very drunk during the making of the track – on backing vocals! It has never been released. However, the German heavy metal band Accept recorded a version of the song in 1979 and released it as a single the following year from their second album, also named *I'm A Rebel*. The band U.D.O., featuring Accept singer Udo Dirkschneider, also recorded a new version of the song in 1998 for their album *No Limits*. Another key song on the (Aussie-released) album is 'Jailbreak' which had been penned by the Young brothers and Bon Scott at the Grafton Basketball stadium in the town of Grafton in New South Wales during a soundcheck back in 1975.

The term 'Dirty Deeds Done Dirt Cheap' is said to have been derived from the popular American kids cartoon show *Beany And Cecil*, which Angus watched as a kid growing up in Australia. Despite tour commitments, the album was recorded sporadically between January and July in 1976 at Albert Studios in Sydney with producers Harry Vanda and George Young. The band would work very quickly throughout the 1970s; they had the energy but not necessarily the time. Most of their 1970s albums were recorded live in the studio as a band; Angus's favourite part of recording was doing his guitar overdubs and it seemed like he had endless ideas for riffs. His notes were often frantic and seemingly out of control (although actually anything but), largely due to his super-charged enthusiasm, but it was George Young who kept Angus in check and knew when it was the right time to introduce a guitar solo into a song. Riffs would pour out of Angus and the band rarely – if ever – did more than three takes. Usually, they'd nail a song by the second take. Sometimes George would give Angus a few tracks to work some guitar solos on and George would then tell his younger brother to try some other riff or lead which Angus would do. Thinking he was done by this point, George would then get Angus to take bits from each riff or lead and merge them into one fat guitar sound. It could be hard work, draining even, but it made Angus a better, more confident guitar player.

Their energy and prowess as a live band certainly helped them record albums so rapidly. Also, they didn't want to record anything in the studio that was too 'sterile' or technical which they'd then have difficulty replicating live.

The band continued to record together in the studio to create a trademark live sound. They felt that by separating the equipment they'd lose the raw style, grit and ballsy energy that made AC/DC work so well. It's that basic approach to music that makes rock 'n' roll what it is. After all, AC/DC are not prog rockers. They kept it simple. As soon as the Young brothers nailed down the basic guitar parts they'd maybe add some guitar overdubs and tinker around with the guitars a little. It was all very intuitive, instinctive, inspired.

AC/DC toured so much in the early-to-mid-1970s that when it came to going into the studio they didn't always have the songs completely written and the demos ready. Sometimes the band would have to write the songs in the studio without any lyrics being written beforehand. It was a tough balancing act; touring and making an album so quickly.

Dirty Deeds Done Dirt Cheap opens with the almost impossibly infectious title track which has one of rock music's most anthemic choruses and a stirring riff that's hard to dislike. 'Love At First Feel' is a relatively obscure yet groovy and upbeat number that continues the band's torrent of cheeky lyrics. There's a strong emphasis on backing vocals on this track while 'Big Balls' is a blast from start to finish; Bon's talking and the lyrical content is hilarious. 'Rocker', meanwhile, comes right out of the 1950s;

Bon Scott in the studio in 1976.
Courtesy of Philip Morris/Rex Features

it's the band's tribute to the likes of Little Richard and Chuck Berry and is a powerfully charged track with some cool guitar interplay. It's undoubtedly a hell of a song and one of the album's stand-out numbers. 'Problem Child' is a raucous noise from start to finish with a fantastically prolonged guitar lead towards the end and another killer chorus. 'There's Gonna Be Some Rockin'' is another ode to 1950s rock 'n' roll and it becomes quite clear at this point that the band had not lost any interest in the music of their youth. There's a sharp guitar solo in the middle, a consistent rhythm guitar, strong drumming with a steady bass – basically all the hallmarks of an early AC/DC track. It's a mid-paced tune that sticks in your head. 'Ain't No Fun (Waiting Around To Be A Millionaire)' doesn't really come to life until about four minutes into the song when Angus splits from Malcolm and the guitar work becomes more interesting but as with most of the band's lesser efforts Bon saves it from a state of mere ordinariness. 'Ride On' is a slow bluesy effort that doesn't quite seem to fit into the right place; an album as electrically charged as *Dirty Deeds Done Dirt Cheap* should build up to a bigger, faster and edgier ending so 'Ride On' would have fitted more suitably around track five or six. 'Ride On' could almost be called a filler song. 'Squealer' has possibly one of the album's funkiest bass-lines, which almost, but not quite, dominates the song; it works well with Bon's understated vocal performance while Malcolm and Evans bring back those nasty backing vocals which give the song some edge.

Dirty Deeds Done Dirt Cheap saw the band sharpen their instruments to create a grittier, harder piece of work than *T.N.T.* or the international version of *High Voltage* which for non-Australians was the band's first studio release. This second international release does not go without its flaws, mind you. The schoolboy humour of the lyrics – though an essential part of the band's sound – does get a little tiring but this album does show some progression on Angus's side as lead guitarist. Evans makes considerable and skilful contributions with the bass offering some excellent creativity while the rhythm section of Malcolm, Rudd and Evans is very solid and a taste of bigger and better things to come in just a short space of time. As with all of the

AC/DC

Bon Scott-era albums (Aussie and international versions), there are a couple of fan favourites ('Big Balls' and 'Jailbreak') as well as all-time classics such as the title track and 'Problem Child'.

Dirty Deeds Done Dirt Cheap saw the band edging that little bit closer to the start of what would become their creative peak. Indeed, it is a flawed album and after repeated listening it becomes obvious that the band had youth on their side, yet with age comes experience. There's no question that at this point it seemed almost likely that the band were going to become something big; something that rock 'n' roll needed and hadn't seen before. Certainly on a musical front they borrowed from their idols whilst also throwing their own traits into the melting pot but there'd never been a live band quite like AC/DC throughout the annals of rock history. By 1976, the band had played so many gigs that when it came to recording a new album there was no better way to make new music than to create it live in the studio. *Dirty Deeds Done Dirt Cheap* certainly has a live vibe and pure energy to it.

Their second internationally released album was issued in Australia on September 20, and in the UK and the rest of the world on December 17. Annoyingly for the more casual fans, but pleasingly for the discographers, the track-listing for *Dirty Deeds Done Dirt Cheap* varied worldwide. However, the album was not released in the USA until April 1981 when they had become an international mainstream rock band; it peaked at Number 3 in the *Billboard* 200 album charts. The album fared well in other countries on its original 1976 release: in Australia it peaked at Number 4 and in New Zealand it peaked at Number 20 while it hit Number 15 in France and Number 50 in Sweden.

The delay in the US release of *Dirty Deeds Done Dirt Cheap* was rumoured to be because Atlantic Records didn't 'get' the record at first. This delay also held up the band's first tour of the USA. When the band hit the road on the other side of the Atlantic to promote *Dirty Deeds*, they had already begun working on its follow-up (to be titled *Let There Be Rock*). *Dirty Deeds* would not be released in the States until 1981 (after Bon's death). The delayed released proved to work in the band's favour as they ventured around America on tour because *Let There Be Rock* is a stronger album. It would prove to be their breakthrough US release. Speaking to Tim Henderson of Canada's *BW&BK* in 2000, Angus explained a little more about the album's delayed release: "We had just finished recording *Let There Be Rock* so the North Americans said, 'We want what's current, so we'll have *Let There Be Rock*'. It was a bit strange, but they felt that they wanted the current thing and they felt it would be great because they knew we were going to be touring in the summer for the first time so they wanted a good strong introduction. And for us it was a good thing too because we were very proud of the *Let There Be Rock* album, especially Malcolm and myself because for the first time we could really feature the guitars."

The Australian version of the album features 'R.I.P. (Rock In Peace)' and 'Jailbreak' while the international version saw those two songs replaced with 'Rocker' and 'Love At First Feel'. The latter was actually released as a single in Australia in January 1977 although it never appeared on the Aussie version of the album.

The Aussie version of *Dirty Deeds Done Dirt Cheap* did include the song 'Jailbreak' which had been released as a single (with 'Fling Thing' as the B-side) back in June before the album's release; it reached Number 5 in the Aussie singles chart. Directed by Paul Drane who had previously directed the video for 'It's A Long Way To The Top (If You Wanna Rock 'N' Roll)', the music video was filmed for the Aussie TV show *Countdown*. The actual promotional music video, however, was filmed at a quarry in a Melbourne suburb named Footscray. The title track was also released as a single in Australia in October and hit Number 21 in January 1977 in the UK and then in 1981 in the USA to accompany the release of the album stateside. The Aussie version of *Dirty Deeds Done Dirt Cheap* featured 'R.I.P. (Rock In Peace)' as the B-side while in the UK 'Big Balls' and 'The Jack' were included as B-sides and in the USA 'Highway To Hell' was the B-side. The title track has become one of their most recognised songs and features a phone number (36-24-36) which is actually the measurements of the "perfect woman." However, the song caused controversy in 1981 at the height of the band's popularity when a couple in Illinois filed a lawsuit against Atlantic Records claiming their phone number (which was just one digit away) featured in the song which resulted in them getting harassed with lots of phone calls from AC/DC fans.

'Big Balls' was also released as a single in the USA, as was 'Love At First Feel', which features on the international version but not the Aussie release; confusingly it came out as a single in Australia in January 1977 with 'Problem Child' as the B-side. It reached Number 31 in the Aussie singles chart.

The success of the album led to more TV appearances from the band notably again on the Aussie pop music TV show *Countdown* where they played 'Jailbreak', which they'd used as the music video for said single.

"I remember the first time I came across AC/DC, it was in an advert in *Sounds* and it was for the single 'Jailbreak' and I thought they were covering Lizzy," Def Leppard's frontman Joe Elliott told respected music author and journalist Phil Sutcliffe in 2010. "It was a cool name, I didn't even know about the double-meaning then. But then I heard the track 'Problem Child' and I thought, *Good God!*"

AC/DC also recorded another video for 'Baby, Please Don't Go' and one too for 'Problem Child', both of which were directed by the Australian director Russell Mulcahy who would go on to direct various Hollywood films, including 1986's cult classic *Highlander* and its first sequel.

The reviews of *Dirty Deeds Done Dirt Cheap* were mostly on the positive side although there were two distinctive camps: those who "got" the band and those who didn't. Meanwhile, future reviews of the album would gain more favour. Writing in *Rolling Stone*, Gret Kot said during the time of the 2003 remasters: "*High Voltage* and *Dirty Deeds Done Dirt Cheap* (1976) find the quintet already sure of its strengths: the guitars of brothers Angus and Malcolm Young bark at each other, Phil Rudd swings the beat even as he's pulverising his kick drum, and Scott brings the raunch 'n' wail."

Critic Robert Christgau gave the album a C+ in his popular *Consumer Guide Reviews* and stated: "Like Ian Hunter or Roger

Chapman though without their panache, he [Bon Scott] has fun being a dirty young man – he almost slaves through 'Ain't No Fun Waiting Round To Be A Millionaire', and 'Big Balls' is fully outrageous in its class hostility."

"Critics can shoot us full of arrows but I don't worry about it," Angus admitted years later to Jacqui Swift of the UK tabloid *The Sun* in 2008. "When we started we never had great reviews. I can show you some of them, they were never pretty. We were called colonial hicks, the Chunder From Down Under, and told we should be on the first boat home."

Like the majority of albums in AC/DC's back-catalogue, *Dirty Deeds Done Dirt Cheap* has picked up more favourable reviews over the years simply because the band's sound has not aged. The rebellious nature of the lyrics, the rough and rugged style of playing resonates with every generation. This album may not have picked up stacks of 5★ reviews for the band but it remains a worthy hard rock album with some outstanding tracks.

Dirty Deeds Done Dirt Cheap has since become one of AC/DC's most popular and enduring albums. It has sold over six million copies thus receiving six Platinum Records and has gained the sort of popularity given to their best-known releases, *Highway To Hell* and *Back In Black*.

The band had already begun touring the UK to promote the album beginning in October at Southampton University in England. It was only days after they finished the *High Voltage* Tour in Holland on October 18. They bulldozed their way through 'Live Wire', 'She's Got Balls', 'Dog Eat Dog', 'Problem Child', 'Jailbreak', 'Bad Boy Boogie', 'High Voltage', 'Whole Lotta Rosie' and the legendary blues stomper, 'Baby, Please Don't Go'. The band then headed back to Australia in December to perform the *A Giant Dose Of Rock 'N' Roll* Tour, which came to an end on the Gold Coast on December 23.

Was there a difference between Bon Scott onstage that fans were familiar with and the Bon Scott offstage that the band had gotten to know? Mark Evans told the author in 2012 for the rock website *Rocktopia* in 2012: "He was probably a little bit different from his onstage persona. The onstage persona was definitely a part of him but [he] was just a great guy with impeccable manners. A very warm soul... That onstage persona was just larger than life. It was a party of Olympic proportions too and you could say I've known people that partied harder than what Bon did and there's definitely something driving them to do that. There has to be some sort of unhappiness or something. I've never worked that out. I know that Bon like most of the guys on the road would suffer points where you get lonely; it's just the nature of the beast."

The tour did not go without controversy which seemed to follow the band wherever they went during the early years. During the Aussie tour, the band had to cancel their planned gig at the Tamworth Town Hall in New South Wales on December 16 after town officials decided that because of their reputation (the saucy song lyrics; their onstage antics and such) they decided not to have the band perform there even though AC/DC had paid a bond to cover any damage that might have occurred. It wasn't enough to encourage the council bigwigs. As stories spread about female fans getting tattoos of the band's name, the almost destructible volume the band played at during their shows and Bon's somewhat wildman image, it was no surprise that their reputation preceded them so even those who had little – if any – knowledge of rock 'n' roll would have at least have heard of AC/DC. Not only that but now that the band had uprooted and moved to England, far-fetched tales of their supposed association with punk rock disturbed many conservative-minded Aussies and so their homecoming tour was beset with difficulties and controversy. In time AC/DC would become known as "the thunder from Down Under" for a reason...

LET THERE BE ROCK
1977

"I could put my finger on the timeline and say, well, Let There Be Rock, *that's where the band started."*

Mark Evans speaking to the author
for *Rocktopia* in 2010

The band were working intensely and remained fully focussed on making it big in the UK and Europe. This intensity was very notable to some members of the five-piece band. "Yeah, I think the infrastructure of the band was the intense part," bassist Mark Evans explained to the author for the rock website *Rocktopia* in 2012. "It came with the band. If you look at the complete timeline of the band it's a fairly brief period but I think it's a very intensive and formative period because we went from zero to a hundred-miles-an-hour in ten seconds. When I joined the band we were playing to like ten people a night and then it just took off because of the national TV coverage. Malcolm and Angus are pretty intense guys. They had a very strong vision for the band. It's not like a couple of brothers start a band and they go, 'Oh right, I wanna go and get some gigs. What are we gonna call it?' It'll take a lot to get your band together; to get the line-up together; get a recording deal and so on."

AC/DC

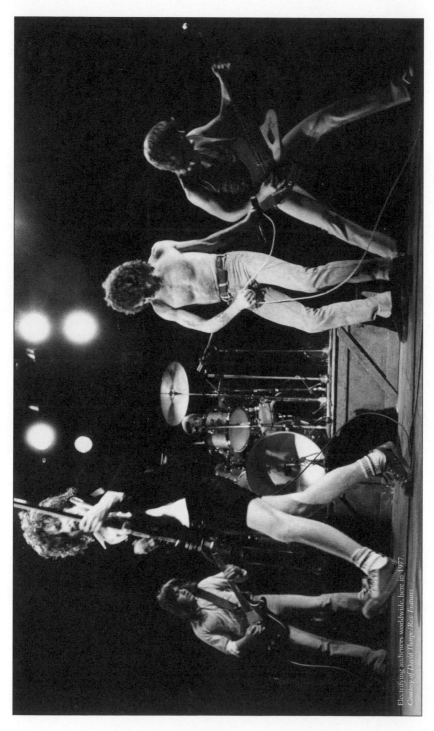

Electrifying audiences worldwide, here in 1977.
Courtesy of David Thorpe/Rex Features

AC/DC committed themselves to another UK leg of the *Dirty Deeds Done Dirt Cheap* Tour beginning on February 18 in Edinburgh and ending in Croydon on March 20. The band's booking agent at the time was the CEO of Epic Records, Richard Griffiths, who was fully aware of AC/DC's onstage prowess.

On March 21, the band's next album *Let There Be Rock* was released; however there was a lull between its release Down Under and the rest of the world during which time a lot happened to the band. On April 3, they performed live on the popular Australian TV pop show *Countdown* hosted by Molly Meldrum – unbeknown to everyone, it would be their last ever performance with Bon Scott on TV. They played 'Dog Eat Dog' from their forthcoming studio album. Right after that they flew to Europe to support Black Sabbath on a tour. Ozzy Osbourne and Bon Scott on tour together would certainly have been the case of who could drink the most pints but for the most part whenever AC/DC toured with another band – and usually those bands were far more established – they'd just keep themselves to themselves.

It was after the tour with Black Sabbath in April that bassist Mark Evans departed from the band. He played his last gig with the band in Germany. He never got to tour the USA because of the hold up on the release of *Dirty Deeds Done Dirt Cheap,* much to his disappointment. The band are famously close-knit and have declined to elaborate on Evans' dismissal.

Mark Evans spoke to the author for an interview on the rock website *Rocktopia* in 2012: "I don't think there was any distance particularly between me and the guys *per se*; I just think that it's just the way they are. There were a lot of times where we just had a ball. We were really good mates. The way I can best explain it is I really do believe those guys were put on this earth – especially Malcolm – to be in a band. Both of 'em – especially when I was in the band – their commitment level was just unbelievable. They're so committed to the cause. They made it really clear about what should be going on; they were very firm about what direction the band should take. It had a lot to do with Phil too.

AC/DC

You were in the band for the band's common good. We were all good mates but there was a time when you were down to business and that's how it's gonna be. We had a night off, let the guards down and go out and have a ball. The relationship was faceted in that respect. Their work ethic and the way they applied themselves to what they did was second to none. It's an unbelievable achievement."

Evans is an important character in the history of AC/DC; not only did he play countless gigs with the band but he also appeared in a bunch of music videos, including the iconic 'It's A Long Way To The Top (If You Wanna Rock 'N' Roll)' and played on the albums, *T.N.T.* in 1975, 1976's *High Voltage* and *Dirty Deeds Done Dirt Cheap* and the band's first masterpiece *Let There Be Rock* in 1977 as well as the 1984 released *'74 Jailbreak* EP (he is credited as 'bass guitar' on 'Jailbreak'). Evans went on to enjoy a varied and accomplished musical career, including spots in Finch, Cheetah, Swanee, Heaven and The Party Boys *et al*.

Evans would never lose his connection with AC/DC. Even to this day, the band play a hefty amount of songs that Evans originally played bass on. He remains an important part of the band's history. Now living in Sydney, Evans is still an active and highly respected musician.

Evans was replaced by Cliff Williams who would also sing backing vocals with Malcolm and Phil Rudd. Cliff Williams was born in Romford, Essex in England on December 14, 1949 but in 1961 the Williams clan moved to Holylake just outside of Liverpool. This was around the time of the highly publicised Merseybeat period that spawned the likes of The Beatles, Cilla Black and Gerry and The Pacemakers as well as many other artists. Williams grew up absorbing not just the sounds of Liverpool but also the Rolling Stones, The Kinks, Cream and of course, blues players like Bo Diddley and Muddy Waters. He formed a band with his mates when he was about thirteen-years-old and like a lot of musicians his age learned how to play the bass by listening to albums and playing them back until he got the notes right. He also took lessons from a local Liverpool musician then left school when he was sixteen. He took a job as an engineer and practiced his music and gigged in the evenings. He moved down to London in 1966 (some sources suggest 1967) to pursue a career as a professional musician but ended up working various odd jobs, including on a demolition site and in a supermarket. He played in various low-key bands but it was when he met future Wishbone Ash guitarist Laurie Wisefield that things started to happen for him. The pair formed the band Sugar, which didn't last long, then in 1970 they formed Home, a progressive rock band that also featured singer Mick Stubbs, keyboardist Clive John and drummer Mick Cook. Home signed a deal with Epic Records and released their debut *Pause For A Hoarse Horse* in 1971 and supported such esteemed artists as Jeff Beck, Led Zeppelin, Mott The Hoople and The Faces. The band replaced Clive John on keyboards with Jim Anderson and released *Home* in 1972 and *The Alchemist* in 1973. Their only hit single was 'Dreamer', which features on their self-titled second opus. Home supported Al Stewart on a tour of the USA in 1974 but Mick Stubbs left the group and the remaining members became the Al Stewart Band shortly thereafter but folded immediately after the tour. Williams then formed the short-lived American outfit Stars and then went on to found the band Bandit in 1974 with singer Jim Diamond and drummer Graham Broad. They released their self-titled debut in 1977 after signing a deal with Arista Records. The band split-up in 1977 after performing as the backing band for Alexis Korner on *The Lost Album*. Frustrated with struggling to find a band that didn't fold or frequently change personnel, Williams decided to stop playing music for the time being.

However, his Bandit's cohort, Jimmy Litherland, suggested he audition for AC/DC. Williams saw AC/DC on *Top Of The Pops*, the once popular and iconic British pop music show, and was impressed by their raw, energetic performance. He joined in four jam sessions with the band in Victoria where they played 'Live Wire', 'Problem Child' and some old blues standards. It's been said that in addition to his obvious musicianship, Angus also thought Williams' good looks would attract women to the band!

AC/DC

May 27 is said to be the date when Cliff Williams officially joined AC/DC. Given Williams' British nationality he initially had difficulties gaining a work permit for Australia where the band were recording their next album *Powerage* but it was a minor hiccup that was dealt with in time.

With Williams onboard, the band had now cemented its most iconic line-up: singer Bon Scott, lead guitarist Angus Young, rhythm guitarist Malcolm Young, drummer Phil Rudd and bassist Cliff Williams. The newly recruited English bassist made his live debut with the band with two shows at Sydney's Bondi Lifesaver in July. His steady but deep and rhythmic bass was perfect for AC/DC's hard blues stomp and it was obvious the band had made the right choice with Essex's Cliff Williams as bassist.

Let There Be Rock, which features Mark Evans on bass and was his last album with AC/DC, was recorded at Albert Studios in Sydney during January and February with producers Harry Vanda and George Young.

Mark Evans spoke to the author for an interview on the rock website *Rocktopia* in 2012: "All the albums I was involved with – *T.N.T*, which is half the international *High Voltage*, *Dirty Deeds*... and *Let There Be Rock* – all those albums were recorded under a two week period. Basically, the songs would be deconstructed and put back together with George, Malcolm and Angus so the whole thing was not only recorded in the first week but written too. That's a hell of a work-load. We did all the backing tracks as they were getting completed. Those albums were all recorded within an eighteen-month period, which will give you an idea of the work the band had and we were doing up to ten gigs a week too. That's why when we landed in the UK after a solid year on the road people would say, 'God, they sound like they've just done 500 gigs.' Well, yeah!"

The band elaborated on an obscure song called 'Dirty Eyes', which was eventually released in the *Bonfire* box-set in 1997, and turned it into what became 'Whole Lotta Rosie'. They recorded a bunch of songs, namely, 'Love At First Feel', 'Dirty Eyes' and 'Carry Me Home', in 1976 for an EP which never materialised

('Love At First Feel' ended up on the international version of *Dirty Deeds Done Dirt Cheap* but not the original Australian version).

The lyrics for 'Whole Lotta Rosie' were reportedly inspired by a one-night stand Bon Scott had once with an overweight woman at a motel while on tour in Australia. However, to her credit the lyrics suggest that she was a great lover. Angus explained to Alan Di Perna of *Guitar World* in 2000: "This girl who was with Bon, she was a fair- size girl … She said, 'Bon, these last few months I've been with 28 famous people.' And she was giving him the lowdown of … different people she'd been out with and whatever. Anyhow, the next morning Bon woke up … the girl thought Bon was still sleeping. She leaned across to her girlfriend, who was sharing the room, and she said, 'twenty nine.'"

The title track is the band's love song to rock 'n' roll which, like many musicians of their generation, saved them from a life of factory work. It's a fictionalised story of rock 'n' roll with the title derived from "Let there be a light…", a line from *The Bible*'s 'Book Of Genesis'.

When asked by *Guitar World*'s Jeff Gilbert about his favourite solo, Angus Young said in 1991: "The album on which we got to do the most guitar stuff was probably *Let There Be Rock*. Throughout that album, there are many guitar solos and many breaks. I really like some of them very much. The song 'Let There Be Rock' was unusual for me. I remember my brother, George, saying in the studio, 'C'mon Ang, let's get something different here.' And every day, he would come in with something different. I had a great deal of fun on that whole album. On the last track, I remember the amp blowing up at the end. I said, 'Hey, the speakers are going!' You could see it in the studio, there was all this smoke and sparks, and the valves were glowing. He kept yelling at me, 'Keep playing, keep playing!'"

Many of the key ideas behind AC/DC's albums came from Malcolm Young whose role in the band is often understated. "Malcolm is the engine room," his brother Angus would say years later to Darryl Sterdan of the *Toronto Sun* in 2011. "And what he does is unique. There are very few guitar players like Malcolm in the world. There's more people like me: lead guitarists. There's very few who say, 'I just want to stand here and play a good rhythm.' Malcolm is a very good soloist. Don't underestimate him; he can do it and do it well. In the beginning, when we used to play bars, he and I would swap. He'd do a solo and then I'd do a solo. Then he just said, 'I'll concentrate on the backing and you can do all the colourful stuff.'"

Let There Be Rock – which many claim to be the album that laid the blueprint for the classic AC/DC sound – opens with the seductive chords of 'Go Down', which is comfortable AC/DC territory but firmer and grittier. The guitar work is more driven than what the Youngs had shown on previous albums while Bon's vocal performance cannot be faulted. 'Dog Eat Dog' is one of the album's most accessible songs. There's an understated blues texture to the track and a kick-arse solo from Angus but it's the melody that makes this song; add that with the catchy lyrics and you've got a killer rock song that's perfect for the live stage. 'Let There Be Rock' is the band's homage to their heroes and for that reason alone it steals the show. The tempo changes, guitar interplay and Bon's seductive vocals make this an absolute classic from start to finish; there's little – if anything – to say about that song that isn't positive. Rudd deserves some praise for his steady, rhythmic drums that propel the song through all its six minutes. 'Bad Boy Boogie' is the perfect Bon Scott vehicle; right from the title and lyrics to the booze-soaked guitars and toe-tapping beat. There's another strong central guitar solo from Angus and if there is one album from the band that shows Angus's progression as a lead guitarist it is *Let There Be Rock*. 'Problem Child' is an infectious mid-paced but heavy stomper of a rocker and 'Overdose' has a steady but progressive riff interplay between Angus and Malcolm while Evans and Rudd keep a typically sturdy rhythm beat going. All the elements of the band come into great effect on this track yet it remains an obscure oddity in the band's back-catalogue. 'Hell Ain't A Bad Place To Be' has gone on to become one of AC/DC's most memorable tunes and an almost permanent fixture in the set-lists to this day; the band have often used it as a opening song at shows. It goes down in the annals of rock as having one of the most powerful intros to any AC/DC song. The album closes with the amazingly enjoyable 'Whole Lotta Rosie' which needs very little explanation. The tempo changes, relentless riffing, the melody and the way the whole song comes together make it one of the band's most compulsive tracks. (To confuse fans, on the original UK album side one ended with 'Bad Boy Boogie', side two opened with 'Overdose' and was followed by 'Crabsody In Blue'. Other versions had the running order listed here, and when it was re-issued on CD 'Crabsody...' vanished forever.)

It could be claimed that *Let There Be Rock* was the band's first rock album for adults and although they still retained their child-like sense of humour, the schoolboy graphics on the first few albums' artwork had been dispensed with and the band had sharpened and refined their sound, creating a harder-edged type of blues rock. There's no question that *Let There Be Rock* marked the closing and opening of two eras for the band; it's perhaps the first album that contains the now iconic AC/DC sound. They had progressed notably as musicians and songwriters and sounded pumped up and ready to explode throughout each of the nine tracks on this opus. Whereas many of the English punk bands were not especially good musicians, AC/DC was a band that was wrongly dubbed punk – they had some punk-ish aggression and angst about them but at the same time they were strong musicians.

AC/DC were certainly growing from strength to strength in 1977 and *Let There Be Rock* is unquestionably the first classic album but at the same time the band had created an aura, a certain mystique around them. Critics struggled to categorise them and the band had acquired just as many critics and enemies as they had fans and even friends. AC/DC proved to be the rock 'n' roll band that would save the genre and its fans from the growing tedium of Yes and ELP; both bands that punk rockers hated with a vengeance.

"Punks liked them because it wasn't dungeons and dragons, it wasn't all fast guitar solos," said singer Joe Elliott whose band, Def Leppard, used to cover 'T.N.T.' and 'Powerage' in the very

AC/DC

early pre-*On Through The Night* days. He continued to tell former *Sounds* journalist and music author Phil Sutcliffe in 2010: "Bon sang from the heart about situations he knew and had lived through. 'It's A Long Way To The Top (If You Want To Rock 'N' Roll)' sums it up for everyone who's been in a band and not made it. I see him in a van with everyone farting and sleeping in the back and him upfront jotting down those lyrics... His words portrayed the band, who they were, warts and all."

AC/DC may not have had any political connotations or social-political angst and anti-authoritative statements in their sound and image because for them playing music is exactly what rock 'n' roll is about. Sure, there was some rebellion to a degree but that band played simply for the joy of playing. *Let There Be Rock* was not a statement about the state of the British or even Australian economy or about the way the British government runs the country or anything like that; *Let There Be Rock* is a statement about rock 'n' roll. It is an album the band had been building up to make since 1973 and there couldn't have been a better time to create this record than in 1977.

It's also the first album by the band that sounds like it was recorded with thousands of watts of electricity and for that reason it is meant to be played *loud*. AC/DC worked fast in the studio and recording an album live was the only way to capture the energy, charisma and uncompromising drive of the band and those key ingredients all come into play throughout *Let There Be Rock*. The importance of this album cannot be overstated and the fact that to this day they still play at least six songs of its nine tracks on tour proves just how strong an album it is.

AC/DC diehards have regularly proclaimed *Let There Be Rock* to be one of the band's most significant releases. It is arguably a rock 'n' roll statement of intent from start to finish and despite the rise of punk back in 1977, AC/DC proved that good old fashioned rock 'n' roll could be just as profound. Which album sounds better in 2012: *Never Mind The Bollocks* or *Let There Be Rock*?

Let There Be Rock was released internationally on June 23, 1977 (it was also released on 21 March in Australia. However, the album didn't actually enter the UK charts until November 1977, spending five weeks there). It fared well in various countries around the world: it hit Number 19 Down Under and in New Zealand it peaked at Number 42 while in France it hit Number 9; in Norway it peaked at Number 37; in Sweden it climbed to Number 29; in the UK it ventured to Number 17 and in the USA it hit Number 154.

The original Australian album cover featured a shot of Chris Turner's (from the Aussie alternative rock band Buffalo) fingers on a fretboard. This was later changed (as was the international release) to a simple but effective live shot of the band which was taken on March 19, 1977 at the Kursaal Ballroom in Southend, Essex. Yet again, there are variations between the Australian and international releases even though the original vinyl pressings of the albums were exactly the same. Atlantic Records removed the controversial 'Crabsody In Blue' from the international release and replaced it with an edited version of 'Problem Child' which initially appeared on both the Australian and international versions of *Dirt Deeds Done Dirt Cheap*. Track six on the Aussie version of *Let There Be Rock*, 'Crabsody In Blue', was eventually released internationally on CD as part of the 2009 box-set *Backtracks* to the keen interest of AC/DC zealots. The various edits, alternative versions and track-listings have frequently confused AC/DC fans over the years.

Let There Be Rock, the international version, was also the first AC/DC album to feature the now iconic band name with the lightning bolt designed by Gerard Huerta. It has become an enduring symbol and one of the most famous icons in rock music. It can be seen on all the band's merchandise and these days kids who are not even fans of the band can be seen wearing AC/DC t-shirts; it's merely a fashion statement. The same can be said for so-called celebrity fans of the band. They wear the t-shirts because they like the designs rather than the band's music.

The catchy 'Dog Eat Dog' was released as the album's first single with the B-side 'Carry Me Home' and in June the now legendary 'Whole Lotta Rosie' was also released on the international market (it had been released in Australia back in

AC/DC

March), which featured a live version of 'Dog Eat Dog' as the B-side. The main single has become a concert classic and has featured in all the band's live releases. When it was reissued as a single in the UK in 1980 with the B-side 'Hell Ain't A Bad Place To Be' it reached Number 36.

Let There Be Rock was certainly the first album to carry in full the trademark AC/DC sound. After years of constant touring and good but not great albums, *Let There Be Rock* showed rock fans that AC/DC was not a flash in the pan. It was the first definitive AC/DC rock opus.

"Yeah, I'd agree with that," Evans attested to the author's thoughts during an interview in 2012 for the rock website *Rocktopia.* "To me, I could put my finger on the timeline and say, well, *Let There Be Rock*, that's where the band started. It sounded like AC/DC before, of course, with *T.N.T.* and *Dirty Deeds...* but that's where they stuck the whole thing down to a fine point. They'd lost a little bit of that whimsical sort of thing. One of the things I love about AC/DC is there's a sense of humour to it. With Bon's stuff there was a sharp sense of humour. It was just funny stuff; very witty and great lyrics. *Let There Be Rock* is the point for me where it starts. It's because the tour before that we were in London and touring around Europe supporting Rainbow and Black Sabbath. We got a sense of what's going on in London [punk rock] which wasn't a normal thing in Australia."

In July, they recorded a music video for the title track at a church in Sydney's Surrey Hills, popularly referred to as Kirk Gallery. The video showed the band's sense of humour with Bon Scott dressed as a Priest and the rest of the band as altar boys. It was a nifty way to promote their music whilst showing off their wacky sense of humour. It was one of Cliff Williams' first appearances with the band in public although the studio version features departed bassist Mark Evans. It was released in October as a single with the B-side 'Problem Child'. It's become a live favourite (often with an extended guitar solo from Angus and audience participation).

Reviews of the album were more positive than what the band

had previously been used to, as critics began to take notice of the group's progression and strengthening sound. "Now there is not a lot of variety in this forty minutes: seven headbangers and one comic slow blues," wrote Phil Sutcliffe in *Sounds* back in October, 1977, "but that's not what you crave from them is it? You know what AC/DC do live. Blow roofs off. Destroy walls. Steamroller the debris into a fine powder. Well, this is the first time I've heard them pack all of that into a record."

In time, this album would be hailed as one of the band's most pivotal releases and would continue to inspire rock fans and earn the praise of music writers. *All Music Guide*'s Stephen Thomas Erlewine writes: "It has a bit of a bluesier edge than other AC/DC records, but this is truly the sound of the band reaching its peak... And that's AC/DC's allure in a nutshell – it's sweaty, dirty, nasty rock, music that is played to the last call and beyond, and they've rarely done that kind of rock better than they did here."

"*Let There Be Rock* is really about as consistent as an AC/DC record gets. Both 'Dog Eat Dog' and 'Hell Ain't A Bad Place To Be' are superb, once again thanks to the great guitar sound here," wrote one reviewer at *Sputnik Music*. "Simply put, this is AC/DC's second best album, beaten only by *Highway To Hell*, and often deserves more credit than it receives. Angus Young's guitar, in particular, has never sounded louder and better than this, and since he is the focus of the whole band, it is only logical that this record ended up being one of the group's greatest achievements."

The album has a long and healthy legacy with *Q* magazine naming it as one of the '50 Heaviest Albums Of All-Time' back in 2001. *Let There Be Rock* could arguably claim to be the most important work of the Bon Scott-fronted albums. It has won fans from other genres of music and, perhaps just as importantly, critics that had initially criticised the band have since praised this release.

The band headed to the USA in July for their first tour across the Atlantic, beginning at the Armadillo World Headquarters in Austin, Texas. Although the band members got along great, Bon

AC/DC

Scott often spent time on his own and would sometimes disappear leaving the rest of the band to wonder where he was. One time the band made a pit-stop in Phoenix to get some fuel having travelled from California on the way to Texas. Scott had met a woman at the airport bar and followed her, which caused him to miss the flight. "Anyway she takes me to this black bar; she was Mexican and I starts drinkin' and playin' pool," Scott recounted to *Sounds* journo Phil Sutcliffe in 1979. "I had a good night, beatin' every [one]." When the whole bar was looking at this white dude beating a black woman at pool, he realised he'd probably better start losing to avoid getting his arse kicked. He left the venue in one piece and made the gig in Austin, Texas.

After touring the USA for the first time, the band headed back across the Atlantic for a tour of mainland Europe and a lengthy road jaunt around the UK. They played to packed houses of various sizes throughout Blighty. *Sounds* scribe Phil Sutcliffe attended the band's gig at the Newcastle Mayfair on October 29. "The crowd was pogo-ing, roaring and chanting 'AC/DC, AC/DC' after that first number. They basked in their own hell heat while soaking in Angus's flying sweat and snot as if it were Holy Water. And the band, who offer the rare combination of wild excitement and consistency, simply gave them everything like Olympic runners going for gold ripping through the pain barrier."

AC/DC headed back to the good ol' USA in November for some more touring. The band were lucky in that they had some support over in the USA with the Michigan rock station AM 600 WTAC. The station's manager Peter C. Cavanaugh arranged for AC/DC to play at Flint's Capitol Theatre on December 5 with the recently albeit briefly reformed Detroit rock band MC5. AC/DC played a blistering set that began with 'Live Wire' and ended with 'It's A Long Way To The Top (If You Wanna Rock 'N' Roll)'.

On December 7, AC/DC performed at Atlantic Recording Studios in NYC which was recorded and later released as *Live From The Atlantic Studios*. "We had done this type of live radio broadcast thing before, in England and in other places," Angus told *Guitar World*'s Tom Beaujour in 1998 about the experience of playing live with only a small audience to cheer them on. "We just looked at it as if it was a live thing except that it happened to be in a studio. It was kind of strange in a way, because as we started playing, people started wandering in and an audience grew. We had cleaners and tea ladies coming in, wondering what the racket was all about."

The live pairing of Angus and Bon Scott was mightily powerful. Certainly it was true to an extent that there were just as many rock fans wanting to see and hear Bon Scott as there were those who wanted to witness Angus's amazing stage antics. AC/DC's incredibly energetic live performances began to earn the band a reputation in the USA as an unstoppable force of nature. At first, some American rock fans thought they were a comedy act given Angus's schoolboy uniform and the band's pub rock image but once they'd launched into the first song and blitzed through soon-to-be classics like 'Live Wire', 'Dirty Deeds Done Dirt Cheap' and 'High Voltage', sceptics soon changed their minds and looked up in awe at AC/DC.

Given all the concerts the band had performed since its inception in 1973, Angus had mastered his unique onstage persona. He'd usually play an extended guitar solo during 'Rocker', often climbing up on Bon Scott's shoulders and Scott would carry Angus across the stage and even into the audience where smoke would be let off from a satchel on his back. Images of Bon Scott carrying Angus on his shoulders while he played guitar have become an iconic part of rock 'n' roll history. Angus would also have intense fit-like spasms during his guitar leads and duckwalk up, down and around the stage.

"He could get you sometimes," Angus said of Bon Scott to *Guitar World*'s Tom Beaujour in 1998. "Some of the things he did, I would simply say, 'Hey now, there's no way I'm doing that.' He was very gymnastic for some reason, perhaps because of the way he was built, and he could easily climb up a P.A. tower and jump off it – and he'd usually try and drag me with him! He'd be going, 'Jump! Now!' My knees would be shaking and I'd say, 'You've got to give me a few seconds to get my nerve up, man.'"

AC/DC

All this happened while Williams, Rudd and Malcolm created a solid rhythm section; a deceptively simple but powerful wall of sound as a backdrop to Bon's vocals and Angus's leads.

"We just try hard to please ourselves really. You gotta do what you do best," Malcolm explained years later to *BW&BK's* Tim Henderson in 2000. "You get lots of people saying, 'Oh, when are they gonna change?' and plenty say, 'Don't change.' We couldn't change 'cause we only know the stuff we like – straight ahead rock and roll, no frills and good performances. The music really is the important thing, that's the bottom line, personally that's all I'm interested in, I'm not even much up for the rest of the thrills of it."

Everything about AC/DC from their image to their sound to their lyrics was designed to appeal to working-class people; the regular Joe on the street. Some had attacked AC/DC for their simple sound; the basic three -chord structure and frivolous lyrics but there has always been much more to the band than that. Simplicity works. Simplicity has endurance. Their lyrics have always been deceptively witty; sometimes charming. They've become known for their sometimes overzealous use of double entendres but for the band such subjects were a fundamental part of rock 'n' roll. The band never wanted to steer away from what they knew best. That's how they rolled.

Angus spoke to *Guitar World's* Tom Beaujour in 1998 about AC/DC's lyrics: "I've always found there's a two-sided thing when it comes to lyrics: someone can call a song 'Sexy Motherfucker', and be accepted, and yet we've been writing all these songs all these years, and while there may be the rare 'fuck' in the lyrics there somewhere, it's all been quite clean-cut. Still, people just make the assumption that we're five guys who've just got our dicks in mind."

They were a band that didn't care what the critics thought. They knew the strongest aspect of the band was their live act; they were like a machine. Totally unstoppable. Were they going to be bothered (remotely) by what a snide or negative critic thought? Of course not. Rock 'n' roll had always been about rebellion.

With a healthy and rapidly growing back-catalogue of original songs, AC/DC's set-list was filled up with some gems, including 'Hell Ain't A Bad Place To Be', 'Problem Child', 'High Voltage', 'The Jack', 'Rocker' and 'Whole Lotta Rosie'. Did fans attend AC/DC gigs to see Bon Scott or Angus Young? Probably both. Scott was improving as a singer with every live performance but maybe it was Angus that fans were there to witness? After all, he was the visual element of the band yet put the pair together onstage and you have an irresistible duo and a powerful live act. AC/DC gigs were incredibly intense, frenetic and energetic performances leaving little time for audience members to breathe, let alone the five guys in the band to catch a breath! With Cliff Williams in the band, the rhythm section continued to provide a taut backdrop for the lead riffs and vocals.

They wound up their second USA tour (following on from the initial summer tour earlier in the year) on December 21 in Pittsburgh. They couldn't wait to go back but there was still a lot of work to do before they could truly establish themselves in the USA. Like a lot of bands, they discovered that you could play to packed venues in one state, say in the South, but be totally unknown in the Mid-West. America is an enormous country and has a massive population. They needed that all-important breakthrough album; live shows and positive word of mouth were strong but just not yet enough. America was too big and getting a hit album on the *Billboard* charts was what was needed for them to make a name for themselves in that country. Good things come to those who wait – and work hard!

AC/DC had now become one of the biggest cult hard rock bands in the music world yet they had thus far been unable to reach mainstream attention, particularly in America. They certainly belonged to the second wave of hard rock bands standing alongside the likes of the legendary German outfit Scorpions, Irish rockers Thin Lizzy and the London lads UFO. The first wave of hard rock bands had begun with the likes of Led Zeppelin, The Kinks, The Yardbirds and Cream back in the 1960s. AC/DC were working hard to stand out from their peers.

POWERAGE &
IF YOU WANT BLOOD
YOU'VE GOT IT
1978

"The only image we've ever had is what we really are. We never cover up anything."

Angus Young speaking to Phil Sutcliffe
of *Sounds* in 1979

Powerage saw the vinyl debut of bassist Cliff Williams. His bass-lines have always been steady but thumping and effective; almost understated. AC/DC's trademark sound is essentially very simple; therefore a guitar-based series of chords and a contrived and unconventional bass-line would just not work. Angus was never keen on Deep Purple-style rock theatrics or ten-minute guitar solos and preferred to keep everything simple. Williams doesn't play his bass as prominently or extravagantly as say, the late John Entwistle from The Who or Jack Bruce from Cream; it would not fit with the band's music. The band's taut, sustained and heavy sound adds more definition to the songs and his subtle but strong bass reinforces this approach.

The band's fourth international album was recorded at Albert Studios in Sydney, Australia between February and March 1978 and produced by Harry Vanda and George Young. It would be the

AC/DC

last Bon Scott-fronted AC/DC studio album produced by Vanda and Young so in that sense *Powerage* would be both the end and beginning of a new era; with a new bassist they would enter the most successful and acclaimed period of their now lengthy history. Even in the early days whenever there was pressure from various sources to try something experimental, AC/DC would vehemently stick to their guns. The Youngs believe that simplicity works; forget the notion that it's the same three chords each and every time. AC/DC knew that the regular Joe on the street would want to list to this music forever; that it is timeless. And underestimate the creativity behind 'simple' at your peril.

They're an album band; they have never made songs just for the sake of having a hit single. They enjoyed working with Vanda and Young because they didn't appreciate the prospect of new producers coming into the camp and attempting to change their sound.

The UK CD version of *Powerage* opens with the sonic boom of 'Rock 'N' Roll Damnation' which could not have been a better song to begin the band's second masterpiece with. 'Down Payment Blues' begins with some striking guitar work and the distinctive bass thumping of Cliff Williams, the band's newest recruit. From the gusty vocals of Bon Scott to the gritty guitar work, 'Down Payment Blues' is an accomplished piece of rock riffery. The sharp guitar attack 'Gimme A Bullet' is just as seductive as the taut rhythm section of Rudd, Williams and Malcolm. Rudd could not have been a better drummer for the gritty hard blues rock of the Bon Scott-fronted albums. His drums really make these songs work. 'Riff Raff' is a rock 'n' roll onslaught from start to finish, ranked amongst AC/DC's finest tracks. It's a sturdy piece of rock with a relentless guitar assault and one of Bon Scott's most alluring vocal performances. 'Sin City' has one of the album's most infectious melodies while 'What's Next To The Moon' commences with a deep bass-line and some great guitar interplay between Malcolm and Angus. 'Gone Shootin'' is the album's most understated song; it's almost forgotten about these days but its mid-paced toe-tapping melody and simple bluesy guitar lead is almost mesmerising in its charming simplicity. 'Up To My Neck In You' is a groovy blues-based number with some rugged guitar work while the explosion of guitars, vocals, bass and drums during 'Kicked In The Teeth' close the album perfectly.

The original UK version didn't feature 'Rock 'N' Roll Damnation' at all, although it was a single. The original UK album had a different running order as well. The reason why 'Rock 'N' Roll Damnation' was omitted from the UK release was because of a rush getting the vinyl to the pressing plants in time for the release so it was replaced with the less well-known, 'Cold Hearted Man', which had been archived by the band and was yet to be released (it would not actually be released again by the band until the *Backtracks* box-set in 2009). Also, the original UK vinyl featured different mixes, most prominently on 'Down Payment Blues' and 'What's Next To The Moon'. The album was later reissued with a different track-listing and mixes.

Powerage declared the band's true intent: to spread rock 'n' roll around the world and for it to have a long-lasting effect on the popular masses. Not everybody got it, of course; the band were scorned by some sneering critics for their supposed lack of originality but *Powerage* was a delight for many AC/DC fans and to this day it remains one of the band's strongest releases. Aside from a little filler, *Powerage* is almost flawless. What had begun with *Let There Be Rock* had progressed comfortably through to *Powerage* and things would only get bigger, better and indeed, much louder, in the AC/DC camp. Is it any wonder that today and in fact since 1978 the band have included a handful of tracks from *Powerage* in their set-lists? Does it come as a surprise that masterful songs like 'Sin City', 'Riff Raff' and 'Rock 'N' Roll Damnation' are hailed as some of the band's greatest creations? The band had truly hit their stride; they were no longer just ambitious young men working the pubs and clubs of Australia. They were a fully-fledged rock 'n' roll monster that was headlining major venues around Europe. An album as electrically charged and gutsy as *Powerage* was not only a salute to the music they were so passionate about but also a kick in the nuts to the punk bands that only wished they were this good. Sadly, magazines like *Rolling Stone* preferred to write about punk bands than AC/DC because there was a political bent to that music which AC/DC didn't have. *Powerage* is perhaps the band's hidden gem; an underrated classic album.

Powerage was released in most countries on May 25 including Australia, making it the first AC/DC record to have an almost simultaneous worldwide release. It was also the band's first album to have just one cover on all various international releases. This made sense – such was the band's growing popularity that release dates, cover sleeves and track-listings did not need to differ in each country. The UK version was nine tracks but the European version was ten tracks, with 'Rock 'N' Roll Damnation' at the beginning; AC/DC discographers were pleased that the original ten-track European vinyl edition featured 'Cold Hearted Man' which was not on any other version and, as mentioned previously, was not released again until 2009's archive collection, *Backtracks* (except for the 1987 vinyl reissues).

The album peaked at Number 133 in the *Billboard* 200 album charts and 26 in the UK. Only 'Rock 'N' Roll Damnation' was released as a single with 'Sin City' as the B-side, which became the band's first hit in the UK singles chart making it to Number 24 in June. However, some original European versions of the album did not include 'Rock 'N' Roll Damnation'; the current CD version is now the standard release.

The band had already begun touring in support of the album on April 27 at Victoria Hall in Henley, England. Angus sometimes relied on ideas from his brother Malcolm when it came to stage performances and trusted his talents implicitly. Angus knew that if his guitar or amp suddenly stopped working, Malcolm would still carry on the riffs standing in front of the drum riser.

"He's [Malcolm] probably got the best right hand in the world," Angus told Steven Rosen of *Guitar World* in 1984. "I've never heard anyone do it like that. Even Keith Richards or any of those people. As soon as the other guitar drops out, it's empty. But with Malcolm it's so full. Besides Malcolm always said that playing lead interfered with his drinkin' and so he said I should do it!"

Reviews of the album were perhaps not as strong as *Let There Be Rock* but *Powerage* has picked up better acclaim over the years. Writing on *About.Com: Heavy Metal*, Dan Marsicano astutely points out that "Stuck between the grimy rock of *Let There Be Rock* and the delightfully evil spirit of *Highway To Hell*, *Powerage* didn't make as immediate of an impression as those two records. It could have been due to the lack of one defining tune; there wasn't a spectacular anthem like 'Back In Black' or 'Highway To Hell.' As far as consistency goes, it can stack up with the rest of their Scott-era output."

Powerage was later hailed as a personal favourite of the iconic guitarist Eddie Van Halen as well as being a cherished album amongst fans not just of the band *per se* but the hard rock genre as a whole. Van Halen isn't the only famous fan the album has attracted: the Rolling Stones' Keith Richards has reportedly named *Powerage* as his favourite AC/DC album. It contains some of the band's most iconic and enduring songs such as 'Rock 'N' Roll Damnation', 'Sin City' and 'Down Payment Blues'. Former Guns N' Roses guitarist Slash has cited *Powerage* as one of his personal favourite AC/DC albums; he often plays 'Riff Raff' on his iheartradio channel, Slash FM. The latest line-up of Guns N' Roses fronted by Axl Rose even played 'Riff Raff' during their *Chinese Democracy* World Tour in 2009. *Powerage* was recorded as if it was almost like AC/DC's love letter to the blues; it could have been made in the 1960s and stood up strongly against any album by Cream or The Kinks.

Its legacy is evidently assured with many musicians claiming it to be one of their best albums and while it may not rank alongside *Let There Be Rock* and *Highway To Hell* as the best of the Bon Scott-fronted studio releases, coming in third place is not a bad spot at all. Since its 1978 release, *Powerage* has become one of AC/DC's most cherished albums with tracks from the album covered by an array of artists. The American singer Mark Kozelek covered 'Riff Raff', 'What's Next To The Moon' and 'Up To My Neck In You' on his solo opus *What's Next To The Moon* while the Canadian cult thrash metal band Annihilator covered 'Riff Raff' on their 1996 studio album *Refresh The Demon*. 'Sin City' is one

AC/DC

of AC/DC's most popular and enduring tracks and is said to be a favourite of Aerosmith guitarist Joe Perry while it's also been covered by Twisted Sister, The Offspring, Great White, Bruce Dickinson and Ugly Kid Joe. Also, 'Kicked In The Teeth' was covered by Nashville Pussy on their *Eat More Pussy* album. *Powerage* was rated Number 26 in *Kerrang!*'s '100 Greatest Heavy Metal Albums Of All-Time' poll.

The UK tour was a great success for the band; their reputation as a mind-blowing live act was now assured. Writing in *Sounds*, Phil Sutcliffe said of the Newcastle Mayfair gig on May 13, "This time they sold out the 2,000 capacity Mayfair and there was talk of two nights on their next, which is unheard of. There was no way I could take notes in the throng of the dancefloor. From the balcony they seethed and bubbled like hot springs. And yet there was no violence in this venue which has seen so much new wave aggro. That seems to be a peculiarity of AC/DC. Where a lot of heavy metal bands draw the chest-thumping gorilla worst out of their fans, somehow these tough Aussies just sweat the good nature out of their crowd."

Much of the year was spent touring Europe in support of the album although some Australian dates in March were cancelled as were some European dates planned for the summer (though the band did tour Europe in the second half of the year). Those who had stuck with the band since they first moved to the UK in 1976 were thrilled that there was more original material being played and filling up the set-lists with such juicy rockers as 'Riff Raff', 'High Voltage', 'Hell Ain't A Bad Place To Be' and 'Sin City'. AC/DC were not to everyone's liking, but there was no pretentiousness about them and everything that was done and said through their lyrics and in person was meant with a sense of humour; with a pinch of salt. They carried their working-class values and ethics with them wherever they went; they were very much a working-man's band back in the 1970s.

AC/DC returned to the USA to play the annual Day On The Green concert series in Oakland, California which had been organised by the famous promoter Bill Graham. The 1978 concerts spanned five sporadic days in the summer. Day one was held on May 28 and included The Beach Boys, Linda Ronstadt, Dolly Parton, Elvin Bishop and Norton Buffalo; day two on June 17 included Steve Miller, Bob Seger, Outlaws, Ronnie Montrose and Toby Beau Band; day three on June 23 saw performances by Aerosmith, Foreigner, Pat Travers, Van Halen and AC/DC; day four on July 26 included the Rolling Stones, Santana, Eddie Money, Peter Tosh, Toots and the Maytals and finally day five on September 2 held gigs by Ted Nugent, Blue Öyster Cult, Journey, AC/DC (again) and Cheap Trick.

Ritchie Blackmore's unofficial biographer and archivist Jerry Bloom says, "[AC/DC] also supported [Rainbow] on the last few dates of the USA tour in August '78. Rumours that Blackmore didn't like them are probably untrue. Whilst he once proclaimed 'AC/DC to be an all-time low in rock 'n' roll' it could well have been one of his usual wind-ups … But by all accounts Blackmore used to quite enjoy watching them and liked Bon Scott, so whatever reservations he may have had seemed to have been overlooked by the time of that '76 tour."

Bassist Roger Glover from Deep Purple who played on Rainbow's fourth album *Down To Earth* in 1979 (and all subsequent albums until the Purple reformation, but was not with the band during the shows above), spoke to the LA radio show *Innerview* hosted by Jim Ladd in March 1981 about AC/DC: "I think they are good at lowest common denominator rock. Not to put down AC/DC's audience but AC/DC's audience don't want any intellectual stimulation whatsoever. They [seem to] just want to be bludgeoned in to numbness. Uncomfortably numb. You've got to try and think about the mentality of the main bulk of people out there. I'm trying not to be elitist in anyway because I don't try to demean a rock audience but I can see what they see in AC/DC. You have a few beers inside you. You've been hard at work all day. What you want to do is go out and get excited and not have to think about anything and I can understand the attraction of that. I don't think I could do it. We get pretty basic sometimes in Rainbow. I try and simplify things. Hooks, the art of production is to try and simplify things in many ways but I like to feel there is at least a depth of something there in our music that you can boogie to or you could listen to and get some value out of as well. Which probably cuts us off from quite a lot of our audience. For instance if we went whole-heartedly in one direction or another we might be more successful or not. I think we are straddling a little bit of a line here."

At the time of AC/DC's visit to the USA in the late 1970s, American rock was undergoing some major changes. AC/DC were certainly more in line with the garage rock bands of the late 1960s such as San Francisco's Blue Cheer, Detroit's MC5 and New York's Vanilla Fudge than they were with say, the successful AOR bands of the time such as Journey, Styx and Foreigner. The other blues-inspired American hard rock band that AC/DC shared such bluesy influences with was arguably Boston's Aerosmith whose self-titled debut came out in 1973 and peaked at Number 21 on the *Billboard* charts. As Aerosmith's popularity rose in the 1970s, substance abuse began to take its toll and their success was on the wane and then came California's Van Halen who took the country by storm with their stunning self-titled 1979 debut as well the technical wizardry of guitarist Eddie Van Halen and the charismatic gymnastics of frontman David Lee Roth. Van Halen became the gods of American hard rock.

Flower Power had died and this heavier brand of American rock that was far more suited to AC/DC's sanctum seemed to have taken over. The timing was perfect for these Aussie rockers to kick America's arse though clearly AC/DC had some stiff competition in the USA.

As AC/DC were making a name for themselves around the world, back in Australia the hard-edged blues band Rose Tattoo had released their self-titled debut album produced by Vanda and Young for Albert Productions. The famed producing duo would also work with the band on their next three albums. These Aussie rockers grew up on English bands such as the Rolling Stones and The Faces, and members of AC/DC and even some of their own fans had recommended Rose Tattoo to Albert Productions, which certainly helped them towards a record deal in the first place. Like AC/DC, Rose Tattoo had made their live debut on New Year's Eve at the famed Sydney hotspot, Chequers.

Back in Europe, during the Scottish leg of the band's UK tour, which was held throughout March/April and into June, AC/DC recorded their now classic performance at Glasgow's Apollo Theatre on April 30. Many of the songs from the set were included on the band's first live album, *If You Want Blood You've Got It* which was released on October 13. The rest of the album is made up of recordings culled from other gigs recorded during their extensive 1978 world tour. It peaked at Number 13 in the UK album charts and Number 37 in the Australian album charts.

It would be the band's last album produced by Harry Vanda and George Young with Bon Scott on vocals. Vanda had played an important role in AC/DC's history not only for his productions but because he'd even given his Red 1963 Gretsch Double-cutaway Jet Firebird to Malcolm which would help create the famous AC/DC live sound to this day. Malcolm had been playing that since he was a teenager. Malcolm stripped the finish paint to reveal the original maple around the time of 1977's *Let There be Rock*. The guitar had the neck and middle pick-ups removed and at one point Malcolm even placed his socks in the pick-up cavity to prevent feedback distortion. The guitar has a worn look. It has become Malcolm's signature guitar. Another favourite of his was his Gretsch White Falcon.

Former bassist Mark Evans spoke to Thom Jennings of *Backstage Axxess* in 2012 about George Young's importance in AC/DC's history: "During the time I was in the band George was indispensable. Not just in the studio, but as a mentor and a guide to how to run things. I think George's influence can't be overstated… Most bands start out just wanting to get gigs, but Angus and Malcolm were writing songs before they formed the band and they immediately started thinking about making records and getting the band overseas. George was a master in the studio and helped the guys along and George was the most astute guy I ever met in the business."

The band's debut live album was almost like a 'best of' release with many of the band's top-rated songs included in the set such as 'Problem Child' and 'Riff Raff'. It features songs from *T.N.T.*, *Dirty Deeds Done Dirt Cheap*, *Let There Be Rock* and *Powerage*. The album offered an excellent opportunity for the band to celebrate their first few releases. Live albums have not always pleased fans; some can tell right away that either the vocals or the guitars have been overdubbed and there's been some changes on the bass or whatever but AC/DC's first live effort genuinely represents the band's fierce live performances during that particular era in their career when they were almost unstoppable. Few bands had the onstage energy that AC/DC had in abundance.

The album was only tinkered with during production in terms of running order, so the track-listing that made the final release does, in fact, differ slightly from what was performed on the night but this doesn't take away from the energy and charisma of the band's performance. 'Dog Eat Dog' and 'Fling Thing' were played on the night in Glasgow on April 30 but removed from the track-listing while the guitar solo during 'Rocker' was edited out. The concert was also filmed visually but never released in full on VHS or DVD, which is disappointing as the band came on in Scottish football attire; yet bits of video have been used over the years and 'Riff Raff' and 'Fling Thing/Rocker' featured on the *Family Jewels* DVD collection and some segments of live footage appeared on the *Plug Me In* DVD set. What's startling about the archive footage from the 1970s is just how little AC/DC have changed since then (the changes to the line-up, particularly the drummers and in the early days the bassists). 'Whole Lotta Rosie' with the B-side 'Dog Eat Dog' was culled from the band's first live album and released as a single in 1978 and again in 1979, which reached Number 47 in the UK singles chart.

If You Want Blood You've Got It opens with a blistering take on 'Riff Raff' before they continue with the electric riffing madness of 'Hell Ain't A Bad Place To Be'. 'Bad Boy Boogie' is perhaps better than the studio version; its meaner and more menacing, perfectly suited to the song's lyrics. 'The Jack' is the archetypal AC/DC song for the audience to sing along to and 'Problem Child' is a simple yet toe-tapping – even head-banging – rocker while 'Whole Lotta Rosie' is much faster than the studio version.

There's some great audience interaction and an excellent vocal performance from Bon Scott. The band keep up the pace and the rhythm section is as taut as anything from their studio albums while the guitar solo from Angus is a killer. 'Rock 'N' Roll Damnation' lifts up the temperature even higher and the band get the audience's adrenaline even more pumped while 'High Voltage' is another classic sing-along AC/DC rocker. The atmosphere is electrifying! 'Let There Be Rock' is one of the band's all-time greatest live accomplishments while the closing track 'Rocker' says it all, really.

If there is such a thing as the perfect testament to the sheer energy, charm and brilliance of AC/DC as a live band during the Bon Scott years then it is *If You Want Blood You've Got It*. These bad boy rockers – all five of 'em, singer Bon Scott, lead guitarist Angus Young, rhythm guitarist Malcolm Young, bassist Cliff Williams and drummer Phil Rudd – were an irresistible live force. The band were already well-known in Australia, the UK and parts of Europe but like KISS with their landmark 1975 live album *Alive!*, AC/DC's first live album would help them gain a much needed foothold in the famously tough American market. Live albums not only show how good a band is onstage but they also serve as a 'best of' collection and the track-listing for AC/DC's debut live release was well-chosen. As headliners of their own tours, AC/DC were unstoppable and as support acts they often upstaged the main bands; AC/DC was one hell of a strong live act. Their label knew this hence the reason behind the recording and subsequent release of *If You Want Blood You've Got It*. AC/DC are one of few bands in the annals of rock history that make their audiences from whichever country around the world feel at home. The band had an amazing rapport with their audiences and this album is a testament to Bon Scott's showmanship and talents. Is it any wonder Bon Scott is hailed as one of the greatest frontmen in rock? *If You Want Blood You've Got It* remains an important cornerstone in the history of the band and the genre.

Upon its release, AC/DC's first live album was greeted with positive reviews as the band had become one of the strongest, most reputable live rock acts of the 1970s. It has since become a firm fan favourite and a highly praised release by critics. Writing on *All Music Guide*, acclaimed American rock author Greg Prato states: "Few others could match the band's electrifying live performances: Angus Young's never-ending energy and wise-ass antics, Bon Scott's whiskey-soaked vocals, and the rest of the band's penchant for nailing simple, yet extremely effective and memorable riffs and grooves."

The album's long-lasting legacy means that it will forever be hailed as one of rock music's most potent live records. Indeed, it is a testament to the band's live appeal and a great tribute to Bon Scott's enviable talent. *If You Want Blood You've Got It* was even rated Number 2 in *Classic Rock* magazine's '50 Greatest Live Albums Ever' poll in 2003.

After finishing the *Powerage* tour in Belgium on October 27, the band began a promotional tour of the UK for their first live album which opened at Essex University on October 28 and finished with two nights at the Hammersmith Odeon in mid-November. The set-list for the UK tour was a fine collection of sturdy rockers: 'Live Wire', 'Problem Child', 'Sin City', 'Gone Shootin'', 'Bad Boy Boogie', 'Hell Ain't A Bad Place To Be', 'High Voltage', 'The Jack', 'Whole Lotta Rosie', 'Rocker' and the ultimate AC/DC live number, 'Let There Be Rock'.

Ever since the band started playing live, an AC/DC gig has always been a sweat-drenched affair. Men and women at those sticky, smelly 1970s AC/DC gigs looked like they'd been swimming with their clothes on. AC/DC attracted a fairly balanced mix of the sexes, unlike, says, the Canadian prog rock band Rush whose audience is often primarily male. The volume of an AC/DC gig was always loud; incredibly loud like military tanks roaming through a quiet country village. Yet the audiences loved it. Playing onstage was what the band did best and they never hid the fact that concert venues were like their second homes.

Beginning and ending the year with touring was how the band worked. It was intensive but the Young brothers had a plan and everything was falling into place. It seemed as though nothing would get in their way. Sadly, things would not work out as planned.

HIGHWAY TO HELL

1979

"Well, the bottom line cobber to answer your question he [Robert 'Mutt' Lange] was instrumental in getting me to project myself."

Bon Scott speaking to Phil Sutcliffe
of *Sounds* in 1979

"All you need to know about AC/DC is this – we stopped growing musically when we were seventeen," Angus explained to Brian Boyd of the UK's *Daily Telegraph* in 2008. "When you're seventeen, you write songs that you hope will appeal to other seventeen-year-olds. And we still write songs for seventeen-year-olds!"

AC/DC have always been aware of the demographic of their fanbase. Although AC/DC's roots were firmly planted in the blues rock movement of the 1960s with inspirations from black American blues masters like Muddy Waters and Robert Johnson and rockabilly players like Eddie Cochran, AC/DC were inevitably categorised as a heavy metal band. Given the loudness of their music and the cocksure image of frontman Bon Scott it is obvious to see why. However, AC/DC are emphatically not heavy metal. Heavy metal's origins are generally understood to have started with Black Sabbath's masterful 1970 self-titled debut. Although the likes of The Kinks, Cream and Led Zeppelin had

AC/DC

an influence on heavy metal with the distorted guitars, heavy bass and pounding drums, they were all blues-influenced rock 'n' roll bands and even Black Sabbath never considered themselves anything other than a hard rock act. Following on from Black Sabbath were the likes of Germany's Scorpions and America's KISS but again, they are not specifically heavy metal. The first band to label themselves as such was undoubtedly Black Country metal band, Judas Priest, who would later create the iconic silver studs and black leather heavy metal image that is now a famous hallmark of the genre. Many observers dubbed them 'the Metal Gods'. AC/DC were rock 'n' roll through and through but they have always appealed to metal fans; and with their 1970s albums they would influence a myriad of heavy metal bands from the late 1970s onwards.

1979 would bring the kind of success that AC/DC had craved since their inception back in November 1973. A scheduled tour of Japan as part of the *If You Want Blood Tour* was cancelled (due to visa problems) while the third leg of the tour saw the band journeying around the USA from April through to August. It was time for another album. AC/DC hooked up with producer Robert 'Mutt' Lange, a decision which would change everything for the band.

As the band grew in stature and their popularity rose in the UK and USA, their record label suggested to AC/DC that it was maybe time they began working with other producers. George Young magnanimously informed his brothers it would be good for them; that the experience they'd gain working with other producers would be to their favour. The label put them in touch with various producers, including the legendary Eddie Kramer who remains famous for his work as engineer and/or producer with the Rolling Stones, Led Zeppelin, Jimi Hendrix and David Bowie *et al*. AC/DC needed somebody who understood their music, where they were coming from with their sound. As soon as Mutt Lange entered the picture it was obvious that he knew what to do with AC/DC's music; how to refine and strengthen it without losing any of its integrity.

The resultant album – *Highway To Hell* – was mostly recorded at Roundhouse Studios in London, England between March and

April, 1979 with said producer and engineer Mark Dearnley. It marked the band's first studio album to be recorded outside of Australia. However, pre-production had begun in January at Albert Studios in Sydney with Harry Vanda and George Young. They'd also recorded some demos Down Under and it was in Sydney where they met producer Eddie Kramer but no songs were recorded and that partnership stalled. It was after that point when Lange was hired and the band set to work on the album proper at Criteria Studios in Miami, Florida in February before moving to London in March. The album was mixed at Basing Street Studios in London.

"We try to do everything with a fresh approach," Angus told *Guitar World* scribe and author Steven Rosen years later in 1984. "We try and get an idea of what we basically want from the album. We don't like to leave people dry or have them say, 'These guys have left us and gone off to something else.' That self-indulgent thing. So we try and keep it basic. A lot of people say we work a formula, but we don't. We try a fresh approach all the time."

Angus has never been interested in complex Jimmy Page style guitar solos, monolithic Tony Iommi-style riffs or long-winded, convoluted chord changes. He prefers clean lead riffs with no frills and no fuss; that's just his style of playing and it's always worked for the band. He worked fast in the studio; he's never been one to break down a riff, to dissect it and analyse it. It was more like a case of a couple of takes and he was done. Neither Angus nor any other member of the band were ever short of ideas. Angus had lost interest in many of the English guitarists like Page, Beck and Clapton; they'd all become too technical for his taste. Angus's main love and undying interest was in American blues. He'd *always* find time for Muddy Waters and B.B. King.

Lange's distinctive sound made an impact on AC/DC, as engineer/mixer Mike Fraser, who later worked with AC/DC from the 1990s onwards, told *Classic Rock*'s Geoff Barton: "It's funny talking to some of the band about Mutt. He did a great job… sometimes he would take days working on a single snare-drum sound … Mutt sure put his influence on it but the songwriting and everything, and the parts they sang and played, came from them."

"I've never been great with harmonies," Angus later confessed to Alan Di Perna of *Guitar World* in 2009. "If I write something, I just tend to mumble and get a rough kind of tune goin'. I'll concentrate more on the swing side of it than anything – the rhythm side."

Working with a new producer such as the then-relatively unknown Mutt Lange was also to the band's advantage because they wanted to try their hand at crafting more melodic and medium-paced rock tracks rather than the in-your-face style rock 'n' roll of *Let There Be Rock*. Lange has made a lasting impression on all the artists he has worked with throughout his career. The Canadian rocker Bryan Adams who worked with Mutt Lange on several albums throughout the 1990s spoke about the producer's talent to Dale Kawashima of *Songwriter Universe* in 2005: "He is an absolutely incredible musician and a very accomplished singer, with a sense of rhythm that I presume he got from growing up in South Africa, but more likely it's just him and his way."

What are the traits of a classic AC/DC song? Well, the first one is obviously rhythm. It's got to rock and the melody has to be centred around a riff. The lyrics have got to be catchy and of course there's gotta be a solo in there.

"Malcolm is a great writer too," Anthony Bozza, author of *Why AC/DC Matters*, told *Classic Rock Revisited*'s Jeb Wright in 2011. "There is an unknown language that happens between Angus and Malcolm and they have this special timing when one hits a chord or a note. I think that happens when you have siblings in bands. Either you have to play with that person forever or there is something genetic between the brothers."

Lange brought a more commercial feel to the band's sound yet the hard rock riffs and unstoppable energy was still present as were the band's witty, lust-filled lyrics. There have been various theories about the direct meaning of the lyrics such as Angus saying the lyrics were directly about being on tour, the gruelling city-to-city, country-to-country schedule that was like a highway to Hell; latterday AC/DC frontman to Brian Johnson reportedly claimed that they were inspired by the dusty overheated American mid-West where the band have toured in the past; other reports suggest that the Young brothers and Bon Scott drew inspiration from the Sydney to Melbourne touring circuit that covers hundreds if not thousands of miles, which is especially tough during the famously hot summers. Certain lines in the song could have come from other sources: reports have suggested that Bon Scott was inspired by his regular trips to a rock 'n' roll-style pub in Perth called Raffles Hotel; there is a road nearby called Canning Highway that was the cause of many deaths because of its bendy structure. The mythology only makes the title even more appealing.

There was also more emphasis on backing vocals throughout the opus and Lange added more grooves and melody. It was the kind of sound that would surely bring them success on the radio and thus in the charts. The band, of course, stayed with their trademark sound yet Lange had somehow made it more fun. The collection of songs on *Highway To Hell* are definitely more accessible to mainstream music fans than what AC/DC had previously created and there is a radio-friendly vibe running through the album, yet it remains distinctly AC/DC and therein lies Mutt Lange's talent; his incredibly attentive ear and his astute sense of music.

The band wanted an album where fans would say, "Yeah, that sounds like AC/DC" but at the same time they didn't want to recycle the same formula which is why it was good for them to hook up with a different producer. It was a challenge for them but it helped them refine and reshape their music as well as grow as songwriters. Throughout the 1970s the band had done something quite exciting with the way they made and presented aggressive rock music; it was a far cry from punk. The AC/DC sound is catchy and melodic but still aggressive and with lots of hooks.

Highway To Hell opens with the trailblazing guitar riffs of the title track before the band launch into one of their most melodic and indelible choruses. 'Girls Got Rhythm' sees the band enter new territory with a melodic mid-paced track that is propelled by the steady drums of Phil Rudd. 'Walk All Over You' is grounded in late 1960s blues rock; the opening lead riff paves the way for a fast rocker while 'Touch Too Much' is a horny little devil of a track and 'Beating Around The Bush' remains one of the album's lesser known songs but it has a seductive charm and a catchy beat. 'Shot Down In Flames' remains one of the band's most striking hard rockers; a terrific song with a robust bass-line that aids the tight rhythm section and a simple yet effective lead riff. 'Get It Hot' is an absolute stomper from start to finish and there's even a nifty little guitar solo from Angus thrown in for good measure. The way 'If You Want Blood (You've Got It)' drags you into the track and keeps your attention for the ensuing four minutes is a hallmark of the Mutt Lange-produced tracks. 'Love Hungry Man' is an understated rocker with some excellent guitars and finally 'Night Prowler' is a suitably creepy blues-tinged number with a fine vocal performance from Mr Scott.

Highway To Hell remains a flawless album; it bridges the gap between the blues rock of the 1960s and the hard melodic rock of the 1970s and it's little wonder this album turned out to be the band's much-needed breakthrough release in the USA. Each track not only carries the famous hallmarks of the band but there's also more melody than had been utilised on previous releases. This was the album that the band had spent the past several years building up to create; with the experience they'd gained from hundreds of gigs around Europe and Australia and the quick jaunts into the studio they now had the know-how to create their first fully-fledged masterpiece. Key to this album is certainly the production; each instrument comes through crystal clear and Bon Scott's voice had never sounded better yet there's still that old rugged working-class charm to his voice that rock fans have found so alluring even to this day. There is an honesty to AC/DC's music and while this album may be their most commercial release of all the Bon Scott-fronted albums, the band had not lost any of their integrity. There are few bands of AC/DC's stature where each member has as much of an important role to play in the sounds of a record; Rudd, Williams and Malcolm are one of the tightest and most powerful rhythm sections in rock history while Angus provides some striking lead riffs and Bon Scott is, well, Bon Scott. There's no question about it: *Highway To Hell* is an all-time classic rock album.

Released on August 3, *Highway To Hell* was the band's breakthrough release and peaked at Number 17 in the *Billboard* Top 200 in the USA, making it their highest charting album in the States up to that point. It was also the band's highest charting release in the UK peaking at Number 8 while in Australia it hit Number 13 and in New Zealand it peaked at Number 37; in Canada it reached Number 40; in France it climbed to Number 2; it hit Number 37 in Norway; Number 24 in Sweden; Number 57 in Switzerland and Number 38 in Austria. Suffice to say the album was a mega-hit by the band's previous standards. Although it had taken the band years, it seemed like all of a sudden AC/DC was one of the world's biggest rock acts. The track-listing was identical on every worldwide release although the Australian and German album sleeves did differ (mostly colour variations).

The bouncy 'Girls Got Rhythm' was the first single taken from the album. 'T.N.T.' was the single's B-side. Of all the band's singles up to that point, 'Girls Got Rhythm' is the one with a pop aesthetic yet it's still edgy enough not to frustrate the hard rock fans. It's certainly a radio-friendly track and could easily stand up against singles by the AOR giants of the time like Journey and Foreigner. 'Highway To Hell' was released as a single (with 'If You Want Blood (You've Got It)' as the B-side) and fared well in various countries; it peaked at Number 24 in Australia, Number 56 in the UK and Number 47 in the USA. It even spent a whopping 45 weeks in the German charts despite only reaching Number 30 in its nineteenth week. 'Touch Too Much' was the third and final single taken from *Highway To Hell* and reached Number 13 in Germany, Number 29 in the UK (earning them a *Top of the Pops* appearance!) and Number 106 in the USA thus securing its place in the coveted *Billboard* 200 singles chart. For the music video, the band simply used a live rehearsal performance from the *If You Want Blood* Tour. The single's B-sides were live versions of 'Live Wire' and 'Shot Down In Flames'.

AC/DC

In truth, *Highway To Hell* was exactly the kind of album AC/DC needed at that point in their career; it was more daring than their past releases and more striking. It was hard enough for the European audiences who dug the likes of German band Scorpions and melodic enough for Americans at a time when melodic rock was riding high with bands like Journey, REO Speedwagon and Foreigner. Given the title, it was also bound to attract heavy metal fans. AC/DC are not, of course, a heavy metal band despite being wrongly dumped in the genre by ignorant critics and the mainstream press. They're a rock band through and through. They're loud and fast but not always heavy; not all the time. AC/DC have a different kind of heaviness too; a heaviness that's bluesy and based not only on riffs but also on the drums and bass.

Highway To Hell was certified 'seven times Platinum' in May 2006. The album's success and longevity is down to the strength of the songs with many of the tracks still being performed by the band in their live shows to this day such as 'Shot Down In Flames', 'Girls Got Rhythm', 'If You Want Blood (You Got It)' and of course the title track. For many rock fans, *Highway To Hell* represents the very best of the most iconic AC/DC line-up: singer Bon Scott, lead guitarist Angus Young, rhythm guitarist Malcolm Young, bassist Cliff Williams and drummer Phil Rudd.

"We started life as a band," Angus said to Paul Cashmere of *Undercover* in 2008. "AC/DC was a band first and foremost. We never looked at ourselves as individual pieces. That has always been the way we have looked at it. I have never said AC/DC is one guitar solo and here is your drum solo. AC/DC is a combination of five guys who all play with the same intent in mind. We go out there to play a bit of rock and roll. We aren't five individual guys displaying their technique."

Almost inevitably, the title track has become one of the most famous rock songs in history and has won various accolades and inclusion in too many polls to list here, including ones by *Rolling Stone* and *The Top 500 Heavy Metal Songs Of All-Time* by the Canadian rock and metal historian Martin Popoff. The track has also been the cause of controversy because of the title and the single's artwork which depicts Angus Young with devil horns, as does the international album cover while the Australian album artwork displays the band members' faces in flames. Inevitably, some people wrongly accused them of being Satanists and Devil worshippers which is obviously and laughably far from the truth.

At first given the rising growth in popularity of the band in the USA, they were a little concerned about how the Americans would take to the album's name but in truth some of the Southern states of American were the first to play the title track on the radio. The album has also gone down in the history books not just for its quality and commercial success but also for the controversial murder cases in 1985 which centred around the serial killer Richard Ramirez also tagged as the 'Night Stalker' by the media who were quick to latch onto the story. He was said to be an AC/DC fan; Ramirez murdered at least a dozen women in the Los Angeles area and was finally apprehended by law enforcement officers on August 31, 1985.

The case brought a high level of publicity to the band in the mid-1980s, much of it negative. They also faced a huge backlash from many parents, conservative groups and certain religious bodies. The song 'Night Stalker' – of course – was not Satanic in the slightest nor about any form of evil; it's basically a cheeky set of lyrics about a boy that sneaks into his girlfriend's house at night while her parents are sleeping. The press, and in particular Tipper Gore and the Parents Music Resource Centre (an organisation that spoke out against profanity and explicit themes in music), were appalled, albeit while losing sight of the relatively benign lyrics.

"Nobody got us, the odds were not in our favour," explained Angus to Jacqui Swift of *The Sun* in 2008. "We didn't have a commercial sound. People were just into very light and user-friendly music and they looked at us and said, 'What is this?'. They'd even refuse to print our photos as Bon was covered in tattoos and that was not seen as respectable."

The likes of Judas Priest and Twisted Sister were high on the PMRC's list and all of a sudden AC/DC no longer stood for

AC/DC

'alternating current/direct current' but allegedly for 'antichrist/devil's child'. Most bands like Iron Maiden and even Alice Cooper (the son of a lay preacher and later himself a born-again Christian) have only ever used imagery featuring the devil and lyrics concerning death and mayhem as tongue-in-cheek ways of entertaining people. It's theatre. Of course, they have no control over how people interpret their music. Even Ozzy Osbourne himself, the supposed Prince Of Darkness, has famously said the only Black Magic he touched was in a box of chocolates. AC/DC have never had any interest in the occult or black magic or whatever; they're more entertained by sexual innuendos and silly one-liners. Nevertheless, with a title such as *Highway To Hell*, AC/DC were bound to upset a certain part of the American population.

Former AC/DC bassist Mark Evans commented on the controversy surrounding the band and their supposed respect for the horned-one. He said to John Parks of *Legendary Rock Interviews* in 2011: "All that stuff came from people outside of the band who had no idea about the band, it's sense of humour or anything else. For fuck's sake they are a rock and roll band, all they do is play music and have a good time taking the piss out of everything. Any other accusation ... is just bullshit. Those lyrics for 'Hell Ain't A Bad Place To Be' are just fuckin' rock and roll lyrics, nothing more, trust me. Bon Scott nor anyone else was into any dumb black magic bullshit, that was just a bunch of people running amok with their own interpretations of the lyric lines. It's rock and roll music but some people felt the need to overthink it."

Reviews of *Highway To Hell* were surprisingly strong during the time of the album's release and to this very day it is a cherished album amongst fans and critics alike. Throughout much of their career AC/DC have been looked down on by the critics although a select few did understand the band and get where they were coming from with the sound and image. Some magazines didn't even bother to cover the band at all and *Rolling Stone* were often snotty towards them (as they were to a lot of hard rock bands). It has always been easy for critics to use

AC/DC as an obvious target of mockery. Given their (supposedly) 'simple' sound and Angus's schoolboy uniform, many critics often poked fun at them right from the beginning. The riffs are direct; the lyrics are frequently silly; so a lot of critics just didn't care for the band at all. Some critics had even knocked Angus's guitar playing! However, the more astute critics knew that AC/DC's sound was not actually easy at all but in fact rather hard; deceptively so.

Writing in *Rolling Stone* in 2003 during the first wave of AC/DC remasters, Gret Kot said: "The songs are more compact, the choruses fattened by rugby-team harmonies. The prize moment: Scott closes the hip-grinding 'Shot Down In Flames' with a cackle worthy of the Wicked Witch of the West."

In Stephen Thomas Erlewine's agreeable and concise review for *All Music Guide*, he states: "This is a veritable rogue's gallery of deviance, from cheerfully clumsy sex talk and drinking anthems to general outlandish behaviour. It's tempting to say that Scott might have been prescient about his end – or to see the title track as ominous in the wake of his death – trying to spill it all out on paper, but it's more accurate to say that the ride had just gotten very fast and very wild for AC/DC, and he was simply flying high."

The album's legacy is quite clearly assured as many fans and critics have proclaimed *Highway To Hell* to be not only the best album of the Bon Scott-fronted records but also the best of all AC/DC's albums. The reverence that has been bestowed on the album has grown stronger with each passing year and like all the Bon Scott-fronted AC/DC releases, it sounds better with age. It has garnered acclaim in many of the worlds' leading music publications and even the mainstream non-music press. For example, *Rolling Stone* (finally!) rated it Number 199 in their poll of the '500 Greatest Albums Of All-Time'. In 2010, the album was listed in the '100 Best Australian Albums' poll.

Given the success of the album back in 1979, the band were on a high; they were feeling good about themselves and were excited by the results of what they considered to be their best album.

AC/DC

More and more people began listening to AC/DC because of *Highway To Hell*.

However, despite the immediate success of the album, the band were still essentially without a permanent base, which recalled those early years sharing the same house in Melbourne. "None of us have had our own places to live for the past two years," Bon Scott told *Sounds* journalist Phil Sutcliffe in 1979. "I rented a flat here for eight months but I was only there for six weeks. All we've got is our parents' homes in Australia."

Angus even told Sutcliffe in the same interview that he rented the flat above Scott's in West Brompton, London. The band members had gotten used to living in hotels around the world, the transient life of a rock star.

The band began touring in Holland on July 13 to promote *Highway To Hell* which took them through to the end of the year, covering much of Europe, North America and the UK before heading around mainland Europe for a couple more legs.

In New York during the American leg, Angus had picked up another Gibson SG (1967 model) that he began to play instead of the previous Gibson which he'd been using throughout the 1970s. Angus also stuck with his Marshall amps. The stacks of Marshalls onstage created a terrifyingly loud guitar sound (and still do!).

"Working for a couple of bucks a week," Malcolm said to Tim Henderson of *BW&BK* in 2000 on the band's thirst for longevity and their incredible work ethic. "Working our butts off getting covered in oil and all the shit that goes with it, and when we got to play club gigs, luckily enough, we thought 'This is IT!, don't have to work. Angus, we can make fifty bucks a week each here, we can survive, without a day job.' That was our big plan (laughs). So everything outside of a club gig is a bonus to us."

Bon Scott's voice had improved considerably during the 1970s due to the constant touring and studio output. There was now an extensive range to his vocal performance; from the creepy vocals of 'Dirty Deeds Done Dirt Cheap' to the melodic nature of 'Let There Be Rock' to the unrelenting speed of 'Rocker'. He could hit high notes, deep notes and offer a wide array of emotions.

The band had a tight set-list during this period and while they changed it to suit the tastes of either the band or the audiences of whichever country they were in, in the USA they nailed it down to: 'Live Wire', 'Shot Down In Flames', 'Hell Ain't A Bad Place To Be', 'Sin City', 'Problem Child', 'Bad Boy Boogie', 'The Jack', 'Highway To Hell', 'Whole Lotta Rosie', 'Rocker', 'If You Want Blood (You've Got It)' and 'Let There Be Rock'.

For many observers, the real drive behind the recorded and live sound of the band has always been Malcolm Young. People obviously know AC/DC from Angus dressed as a schoolboy but the understated playing and image of Malcolm is absolutely integral and lies at the heart of AC/DC. The rhythm is the soul of the band's music and Malcolm has never been afraid of saying what he thinks. He is a vocal critic of the band, often telling Angus if he feels his playing is not up to scratch. There were times back in the 1970s when Malcolm would pick up a lead guitar and play and even churn out a riff, but Malcolm preferred to stand back and play rhythm so he'd drop the lead solos and let Angus get to work.

AC/DC had an enormous impact on the New Wave Of British Heavy Metal (NWOBHM) which had begun in 1979 after the demise of the punk movement. Bands from all over the country formed and began making metal, drawing inspiration from earlier bands like Led Zeppelin, Deep Purple and Black Sabbath to mid-1970s bands such as Judas Priest and Scorpions. Taking tips from the dreaded punk movement, which most – if not all – metal fans detested, the NWOBHM bands approached their music with a sense of DIY. Whereas the punk bands were hardly united, the NWOBHM bands were like a brotherhood even though many of them didn't know each other. Certainly the fans were in brothers in arms, showing off lists of bands on their makeshift rock t-shirts and denim jackets. *Sounds* championed the movement which Editor Alan Lewis had named and journalist Geoff Barton written about so vehemently. With the notable exception of Def Leppard, a band that wasn't exactly metal at all and did their most to distance themselves from the movement, many other bands were proud to be getting so much publicity. The NWOBHM would have a monumental and lasting effect on metal with the various subgenres it spawned such as thrash. However, we're getting a little ahead of ourselves here… what was AC/DC's influence on the NWOBHM? Certainly, bands like Diamond Head, Girlschool and Raven owed a debt or two to AC/DC's fiery brand of hard blues-inspired rock.

"Yes a little," says Diamond Head's Brian Tatler when asked by the author if AC/DC had an effect on the NWOBHM. "It [AC/DC's sound] was very raw, a bit like punk rock so it gave guys like me confidence to have a go. The sound [that] bands like Led Zep and Deep Purple made seemed so far from what I could achieve. It was very encouraging when punk rock bands got signed and indeed when I saw a band as great as AC/DC who seemed very simple and direct in their approach."

Jess Cox of the North East band Tygers Of Pan Tang told the author: "The first time I came across AC/DC was in 1978 at a friend's house. He was an anorak, sadly, and played music 'at you' not 'for you' and if he could get you into his room he would make you sit on a chair and force you to listen to all his albums at volume max. You weren't allowed to talk (not that you could at that volume anyway). Neither were you allowed to touch the records or the sleeves for that matter. You had to sit there and look impressed. Painful as this was (depending if you were into Camel, Hawkwind and Mountain) – I wasn't! – like an epiphany one day he pulled out a sleeve that looked much more interesting. A schoolboy with a guitar through his chest. AC/DC was about to enter my world. *If You Want Blood* it was called. Brilliant! It was getting better by the second and with the first power riff of 'Whole Lotta Rosie' as he expertly dropped the needle cock on the opening as only a veteran Mono Dansette owner could, my fate was sealed. Who the fuck is this! No fiddly-diddle-elves-in-the-forest lyric here … A young man's obsession. So hard-rock-shagging-fun-music… it was all starting to fall into place.

"A year later and I now had my own record player. I remember coming home with my new purchase of the latest AC/DC album and one of the greatest rock albums in the world ever – *Highway To Hell*. I must have nearly worn the grooves out in the first month. I could not believe something could be so exciting. The riffs were out of this world and the songs just pounding pieces of rock you could not keep still to. I was now definitely a fan. I was even in a band now called the Tygers Of Pan Tang; what did we play (as we had no songs of our own at this time) but AC/DC's 'Whole Lotta Rosie'. I could even be Bon Scott now and girls wanted to shag me! Result!"

From October to December AC/DC journeyed around Europe on an extensive tour which included four nights at the Hammersmith Odeon from November 1 to November 4. The set-list consisted of 'Live Wire', 'Shot Down In Flames', 'Hell Ain't A Bad Place To Be', 'Sin City', 'Problem Child', 'Walk All Over You', 'Bad Boy Boogie', 'The Jack', 'Highway To Hell', 'Girls Got Rhythm', 'High Voltage', 'Whole Lotta Rosie', 'Rocker', 'If You Want Blood (You've Got It)' and 'Let There Be Rock'. The tour also included AC/DC's high profile support slot to The Who at Wembley Stadium!

Mike Newdeck, a writer for the melodic rock magazine *Fireworks*, told the author: "Certain experiences and events in your life are remembered forever. Your first love, your first kiss, driving your first car or cradling your first born child all leave an indelible mark in your mind ... and going to an AC/DC concert at the tender and highly impressionable age of fifteen ranks as one such experience. It was 1979; Margaret Thatcher was in her first year of office with the 'Winter Of Discontent' still fresh in the mind, the Three Mile Island nuclear disaster took place in America [and] *The Life Of Brian* was showing in cinemas. The music landscape played host to the likes of Blondie and The Boomtown Rats whilst the New Romantic genre was in its embryonic stages and punk rock was embedding itself in the British psyche. Not the ideal environment for a bunch of Australian [rockers] and their brand of hard rock twelve-bar boogie then? Well, think again!

"Touring the newly released *Highway To Hell* album and selling

Supporting The Who at Wembley in August 1979.
Courtesy of Richard Young/Rex Features

out just about every venue (this was the second night of four at the Hammersmith Odeon), AC/DC joined forces with the New Wave Of British Heavy Metal movement to thumb its collective nose at the punk movement that had become the standard bearer for a majority of music publications at the time. Indeed the night's pairing of AC/DC with support band Def Leppard provided the perfect antidote. It was one of those nights that as a concert virgin you come totally unprepared for; the noise, the intimate atmosphere and of course the velvety flip-up seats that characterised the Hammy Odeon, all became embedded in the grey matter forever. AC/DC was the perfect fit for the Hammy and although they went on to dominate stadia the world over, to many, me included, this was their domain. The closeness of the band to the crowd gave the impression that they were playing for you and only you. Spirited opener 'Live Wire' and other live staples 'Whole Lotta Rosie', 'The Jack' and 'Sin City' fitted seamlessly with the newer material such as 'Shot Down In Flames', 'Highway To Hell' and 'If You Want Blood...' with Angus at the peak of his powers of animation and sheer physical energy; the rock music equivalent of a Tasmanian devil. All the while he was charismatically supported by vocalist Bon Scott's ... banter with the crowd and the metronomic back beat triumvirate of Young (Malcolm), Rudd and Williams."

Newdeck continues: "Angus's walkabouts are legendary and I was entranced by it as the guitarist pierced the crowd with that famous Gibson SG. It was almost biblical, like a latterday Moses dividing the sea of sweaty head-banging mops, eventually making his way onto the upper balcony section during 'Bad Boy Boogie', playing very close to the edge as the rest of the band continued their unrelenting cranium crushing riff. It was craziness and the health and safety brigade would have had a field day. Thankfully they didn't exist in 1979. Yes, this was a show to end all shows, culminating in a raucous version of 'Let There Be Rock' as an encore that no one wanted to end.

"It' been a long time since I was fifteen and since then I have attended thousands of concerts and been entertained by some great bands. However I can safely say that not one has left me with the same feeling as the one on November 3, 1979, not one has left me with a warm glow of smug satisfaction thirty three years later that to this day reminds me that I was part of something really special."

Rob Evans – a writer for *Powerplay* and *Classic Rock Presents AOR* magazines – was also another fan that managed to catch AC/DC on the *Highway To Hell* Tour, this time at the Liverpool Empire on November 6. He spoke to the author about his memories of witnessing the band in action: "For someone that was weaned on a diet of stodgy classic rock, the sound of AC/DC was an acute, jarring blast to the senses – if truth be told, I didn't take to them on first listen. The offending item in question was a two-track 12" single by the name of 'Rock 'N' Roll Damnation', backed with 'Sin City' and it didn't sit well with this young buck. Its punk/metal hybrid of sounds was unlike anything I'd ever listened to at the time. But its blitzkrieg of high octane rock 'n' roll grew on me just enough to buy the album (*Powerage*) and a love affair was born. This was ... a few months after the album's release in January. Over the course of the next twelve months the band would release their seminal live album *If You Want Blood* before hitting the public hard with *Highway To Hell*, an album that was to be the springboard that would take them from pub rock wannabes and turn them into global superstars, but at a cost. When the *Highway To Hell* Tour rode into Liverpool and decamped itself at the Empire Theatre on Bonfire Night in 1979 for a brace of shows, the night sky wasn't the only one to witness fireworks that evening. I actually caught the show on the following night and I seem to recall being disappointed at the set length – a mere eighty minutes – but with the kind of energy on display that could light up the national grid, there was no way they could have done any longer. From set opener 'Live Wire' through to the gig's conclusion of 'Let There Be Rock' this was a sweat-soaked explosion of musical fireworks. Led by Bon Scott, and the human pinball that is Angus Young, I don't think that I've ever seen such an energised performance and quite how Angus managed to keep going for thirty minutes, never mind eighty, was beyond me."

When the band ventured to Paris, France on December 9 they stopped at the Pavillon de Paris to play a show which was recorded and later released as *Let There Be Rock: The Movie – Live In Paris*. It had been a whirlwind year and it seemed like nothing could stop the seemingly triumphant AC/DC. Sadly, fate, if you believe in it, was about to deal a twisted set of cards.

THE TRAGIC DEATH
OF BON SCOTT
1980

"The first emotion I had was total shock. I mean, we knew things with Bon were wild and hectic, but they always were. It was not a situation that I perceived to be life-threatening."

Angus Young speaking to Tom Beaujour
of *Guitar World* in 1998

On January 25 and January 27, following several fantastic shows in France throughout the first month of 1980, AC/DC played two rescheduled gigs at the Newcastle Mayfair and Southampton Gaumont, which were initially planned for the end of 1979 as part of the famed *Highway To Hell* UK Tour. Due to a fire the Newcastle gig was called off although it is unknown why the initial Southampton gig didn't go ahead originally as planned. The Sheffield band Def Leppard – who were hot on the heels of their debut album *On Through The Night* – supported AC/DC on the entire UK leg but presumably because they were making their second studio opus *High 'N' Dry* they were unavailable for the rescheduled 1980 Newcastle and Southampton shows.

Instead, a young metal band from Stourbridge in the English Midlands was invited. Having played just over thirty shows,

AC/DC

Diamond Head were still relatively inexperienced but they were talented and enthusiastic. They were also AC/DC fans and had grown up on a steady diet of hard rock and heavy metal.

Diamond Head guitarist and co-founder Brian Tatler recalls an interesting anecdote on the tour: "We arrived at the venue for our soundcheck and began carrying our gear in various boxes and bread crates. AC/DC didn't show up for a soundcheck. Their crew did it for them, so that left us plenty of time to do one. Duncan started with his first tom *dum, dum, dum* and their engineer said: 'It's a bit out of tune.'

Dunc scrabbled around for a drum key, turned a few lugs, *dum, dum, dum* and the engineer said: 'That's worse than it was the first time.'

Duncan would say, 'Yeah I know it's this drum key...'

A bit more fiddling, *dum, dum, dum* and the engineer then said: 'Hey guy, why don't you go and get a drink? We'll get one of our guys to look at it for you.'

So Phil Rudd's drum tech did all the tuning, dampening and soundcheck for Duncan – [all] very cool! AC/DC had 5K of monitors which seemed incredible to us at the time. I don't think we had played a gig before with a 5K PA."

An AC/DC fan through and through, Tatler continues: "We hit the stage to 3000 rock fans who really warmed to us. We thought, *This is how it works. This is the real thing!* After that reaction we thought the world was our lobster. It was like a glimpse of what could be. I saw Bon Scott watching us from the side of the stage and he gave Duncan his bottle of Jack Daniel's when we came off. *Rippah!*

Afterwards we had a chat backstage with AC/DC's then-manager Peter Mensch ... he seemed to know exactly how the business worked and kept saying, 'The trick is...' It is a shame he didn't offer to take on the management of Diamond Head there and then!

"I can't remember too much about Southampton, other than it was sold out and [famed rock photographer] Robert Ellis was there taking pictures of us. Duncan remembers as he got up behind his kit accidentally kicking over a pint glass of cola and it went straight into the stage box. He was looking at it frothing away while he was playing thinking, 'Oh my God, the PA's gonna blow up!'"

Tatler remembers first meeting AC/DC before his own band found fame as the inspiration behind Metallica, Megadeth and their thrash metal peers. "While Duncan Scott [DH drummer] was working as a glass engraver at Webb Corbett [in the Midlands] he decided to engrave AC/DC onto a blue glass goblet and take this with him to a gig; he showed it to the security and they took us backstage to meet all of AC/DC on the *Powerage* tour at the Birmingham Odeon ... They were very impressed with Duncan's handiwork, it was brilliant to meet them and we all got autographs, including Bon Scott's. When we supported them in January, 1980, we asked them if they remembered us giving them a blue glass goblet. They did remember and Cliff Williams said it was on his mum's telly! A roadie said he had Michael Schenker's actual Flying V in its case that Schenker had just smashed up, and this roadie was going to get it repaired. I insisted he show me and I managed to nick the black and white truss rod cover when he wasn't looking, which I kept for years. We were invited to a party at Bon Scott's flat the following evening, so we got his address and drove around London trying to find it, imagining that all of AC/DC would be there as well as loads of other interesting people. We thought it would be cool to stand around drinking with Bon and the lads, but we could not find the place and eventually decided to leave it and so we drove home."

Roaring on, AC/DC duly wound up the *Highway To Hell* Tour on January 27 in Southampton, England and had already begun preparations for their next album with producer Mutt Lange to be titled *Back In Black*. Yet unbeknown to everyone at the time, it would be AC/DC's last gig with Bon Scott...

On February 18, Bon Scott went to a gig at London's Music Machine Club with pals and the following morning was found unconscious by a friend, who immediately rushed him to King's College Hospital in Camberwell where he was pronounced dead on arrival. Bon Scott was just thirty three years old.

AC/DC

"By the way he carried himself, you really thought that Bon Scott was immortal," Angus Young told Tom Beaujour of *Guitar World* in 1998. "He would drink like a fish, and when you saw him the next morning, he'd be no worse for wear. And you'd think to yourself, 'How does this guy do this?'"

Bon Scott lived a wild lifestyle; it seemed as though he was not afraid of anything. It was the way he led his life and he enjoyed it; he lived for the present. His death has been well-documented over the years in many books and articles; as is often the case with people in the public eye who die young, there have been a number of theories over the years. However, as stated in the Introduction to this book, this is not the tome to investigate the circumstances surrounding his death any further. The facts are that Bon Scott's official cause of death was stated as acute alcohol poisoning.

So what was the real Bon Scott like, offstage?

"It's not unusual for people to have very different public and private personas, obviously there are different facets of people," said former bassist Mark Evans to Thom Jennings of *Backstage Axxess* in 2012. "Onstage you become bigger than life and Bon knew that he had a responsibility to keep that up. What is surprising about Bon is that offstage he was very domesticated, he liked to clean and used to divorce himself from the band when we were off the road so he could do his own thing. Everybody has this idea of the wild-eyed rock and roller, which was part of it, and even later that satanic thing the guys got messed up in which is odd to me and runs contrary to what I think of the guys. He was just a warm guy."

"With Bon he'd just do things off the cuff," Evans then recounted to the author during an interview for *Rocktopia* in 2012. "I remember one night we were stranded at our hotel at a place called Freeway Gardens Motel in Melbourne. It was like serviced apartments and it was cold; it was winter and his apartment was on the third floor and we're up there drinking. It was fuckin' freezing and this guy says, 'It would be great to jump from here into the pool down from the third floor.' And

Bon Scott taking a break during rehearsals, 1980.
Courtesy of News Ltd/Newspix/Rex Features

A genuine rock legend, here on stage at Wembley in 1979. Courtesy of Andre Csillag/Rex Features

Bon said: 'I'll bet you ten bucks.' He swan-dived straight into the pool! It was 3 a.m. in the morning!

"Another time we were rehearsing near an ice rink and I thought he's goin' to go on there and be like a Giraffe on ice skates. He took off. He could ice skate like a genius. He did these things you didn't know he could do. He was just a great guy. I think it's normal when you lose someone like that at a relatively early age [that] they grow in stature. It's bound to happen because the input stops and so it's up to people to pump it up. I've gotta tell you I don't see anything in Bon's voice or his spirit that's not right. He was a genuine guy. It was just a matter for the rest of the world to catch up with it. He was just your real Scots-Aussie and a great guy to be around. It's funny because you expect him just to walk through the door because his image is still very much with us because of all the videos and pictures. He was a wonderful, warm guy. I think he felt a very strong duty to his image which knocked him around a bit. That was all part of the guy. What a frontman. You can tell I'm a bit of a fan."

Phil Ashcroft, a rock enthusiast and writer for the specialist melodic rock magazine, *Fireworks*, remembers seeing Bon Scott and AC/DC seven or eight times throughout the 1970s. He told the author: "I saw AC/DC several times between 1977 and 1980, mostly in Manchester and Liverpool, but I also remember one of their early gigs being at the Floral Hall in Southport. One of the most memorable was the Liverpool Empire show in early 1978, which had possibly the best atmosphere of any AC/DC gig I can remember. They started with 'Riff Raff' from *Powerage*, which wasn't even out yet, and finished with 'Let There Be Rock', which just about brought the roof down. AC/DC shows at that time were quite short – seventy minutes or so – but the energy that Angus and Bon Scott put into the show was incredible, with the chants of 'ANGUS! ANGUS!' starting up as soon as they finished a song. There were no fillers in the set whatsoever and the energy levels were kept up throughout the show. I think this tour was the last one where they played a single date in Liverpool and Manchester, the band going on to play multiple dates on the next tour before stepping up to larger theatres by 1980."

AC/DC

Bon Scott's ashes were buried by his family in Fremantle, Western Australia where he and his family emigrated to as a boy. Naturally, the gravesite has become a cultural landscape and one of the most visited places in Australia. The National Trust Of Australia has since included it in their list of classified heritage places. On July 9, 2006, the plaque was stolen from the gravesite but has since been returned back to normal.

AC/DC had not only lost their singer on February 19, 1980, but rock 'n' roll had lost someone truly special...

BACK IN BLACK –
A TRIBUTE
TO BON SCOTT
1980-1981

"I suppose when we decided to continue, Brian was the first name that Malcolm and myself came up with, so we said we should see if we can find him."

**Angus Young speaking to Tim Henderson
of *BW&BK* in 2000**

Led Zeppelin called it quits when drummer John Bonham died on September 25, 1980; Metallica continued when their bassist Cliff Burton was killed in a coach crash. It's a very personal decision – could a band continue after the tragic premature death of a member? AC/DC were like a street gang so Scott's death had left a huge void in the band. A tough decision had to be made. And would AC/DC ever be the same again, should they carry on?

After some quiet moments and careful thought, the band decided to solider on and find a new singer. They felt that Bon Scott would want AC/DC to continue and with the blessing of his family the band sought out a new frontman. "The worst time was the death of Bon because we didn't know whether we should continue," said Angus to Scott Kara of *New Zealand Herald* in 2010. "Bon's father grabbed me and Malcolm and said, 'Listen, you guys are young guys, so you've got to keep going.' So that took a bit of pressure off us in a way because at the time we felt we didn't know which way it was going to go, because you might be seen as grave-robbing or something."

Also, the band had come up with ideas and new songs before Bon Scott had joined in October 1974 so deep down they knew they could go on with another singer even though they did not want to tarnish the memory of their friend.

Various ideas were thrown round as to whom they could hire, including Noddy Holder of Slade, Terry Slesser formally of Back Street Crawler, Buzz Shearman formally of Moxy and supposedly former Fraternity vocalist, Jimmy Barnes. Barnes was friends with Bon Scott and knew the Young brothers and had even gone into the studio to watch them record with Vanda and Young. However Barnes spoke to *Classic Rock*'s Dave Ling in 2012 about this ultimately false rumour: "The whole thing was a complete urban myth – I never even spoke to the guys about it."

A replacement was ultimately found in Geordie singer Brian Johnson. Bon Scott had come across Brian Johnson fronting the North East rock band Geordie when his former band Fraternity supported them prior to joining AC/DC and was mesmerised by Johnson's voice – liking him to his idol, Little Richard. Bon Scott even mentioned Brian Johnson to Angus back in Australia years previously when they were watching an old tape of Little Richard performing, which reminded Scott of the Geordie singer.

When the Young brothers decided they were going to look for another singer to replace the late Bon Scott, Brian Johnson was a name that sprung to mind, even more so after a fan from Cleveland sent a tape to AC/DC's manager Peter Mensch of Brian Johnson performing onstage. Other people had spoken of him too, including Mutt Lange; everyone seemed to have been impressed with Johnson's performances. What the Youngs did not want was a Bon Scott clone.

Brian Johnson was born on October 5, 1947 in Dunston, Gateshead in England. His dad, Alan Johnson, was a Sergeant Major for the British Army's Durham Light Infantry and later become a coal miner. His mum, Ester De Luca, was of Italian descent. Brian was born the eldest of four children, including a brother Maurice and a sister Julie. Johnson had an interest in singing from very early on and sang at the school choir and also for the Boy Scouts. His first band was the Gobi Desert Canoe Club and a later band he was in was called Fresh. There was even a glam side to Johnson just as there was with AC/DC in the early days: Johnson sang in The Jasper Hart Band from about 1970 onwards. They performed songs from the musical *Hair* and also covered some of the soft rock of the time. Geordie, Johnson's best known pre-AC/DC band, was formed with some members of The Jasper Hart Band.

Geordie was formed in February 1972 with guitarist Vic Malcolm, bassist Tom Hill, drummer Brian Gibson and singer Johnson. In December, 1972 they scored a Top 40 hit with 'Don't Do That' while their debut album *Hope You Like It* was released in March the following year. Artists like The Sweet, Slade and David Bowie were very popular at the time and Geordie tried to enjoy the success of glam rock. They had a number of Top 40 hits, including 'All Because Of You', 'Can You Do It' and 'Electric Lady' and also appeared on TV, notably on *Top Of The Pops*. The band's second studio opus *Don't Be Fooled By The Name* did not spawn a significant hit single and after 1976's *Save The World*, Brian Johnson left for a solo project. He recorded only one single, 'I Can't Forget You Now', which was released in January, 1976, via Red Bus. 1978's *No Good Woman* included three previously unreleased tracks with vocals by Johnson and fresh tracks with the band's new singer Dave Ditchburn. Johnson went on to front a new line-up of Geordie and even signed a record contract in the spring of 1980 but then the call from AC/DC came and the band ultimately split-up.

In March, 1980, Brian Johnson auditioned for AC/DC in London by singing 'Whole Lotta Rosie', the classic track from *Let There Be Rock* and also the Ike and Tina Turner song, 'Nutbush

AC/DC

City Limits'. The band didn't initially know Johnson was there to audition; he was apparently just hanging about with some mates playing pool. He looked like a regular guy who at the time was working on a car assembly line. He had a twelve-year-old daughter and had moved back to live with his folks in the Gateshead village of Dunston. He had even set up his own little company called North East Vinyls, fitting windscreens and repairing car roofs and such. Anyhow, Malcolm finally asked him what he was doing there and he said he was hoping to audition for AC/DC. Coming from a working-class background and inspired by American rock 'n' roll and the British blues boom, Johnson had enough in common with the Young brothers for them to hit it off and they became friends straight away. It's a good job Johnson had made the trip down south. "In the end, I only went 'cos I had other work lined up in London, a Hoover advert jingle!" he later confessed to one interviewer at the *Scotsman* in 2009. "That ad got me 350, the most money I'd had in one go in me life! It's the new Hoover, ooh! She such-a-sweet little movurgh, ooh, yeargh!"

On April 1, 1980, the news that Brian Johnson was the new singer for AC/DC was made official. A new era for AC/DC had been launched. "You know the first thing Angus and Malcolm said to me when I joined this band?" Brian Johnson told *Creem*'s Sylvie Simmons in 1982. "They said, 'Do you mind if your feelings ever get hurt?' And I said, 'Why?' And they said, 'Because if you're going to join this band you're going to be expected to take fucking stick. Because we've been slagged off by every fucking reporter since we left Australia.'"

With Brian Johnson, the band had found somebody who was unique, akin to the way Bon Scott was a one-off, totally different from any other frontman of his era; somebody with a distinctive voice, a strong accent, a memorable look and powerful stage presence. Johnson had some big shoes to fill but he brought his own individualism to the band. Malcolm and Angus had been understandably very down right after Bon Scott's death so when they decided to carry on writing songs, Brian Johnson was the right character to fit into the band's working-class rock 'n' roll ethics. Nobody else could have done a better job. The newly amended line-up also helped distract the grieving band from constantly thinking about Bon Scott's death.

The band headed to Compass Point Studios in the Bahamas a few months after Scott's death to record *Back In Black*. Songwriting, which had begun with Bon Scott, was completed prior to heading into the studio. While the Young brothers composed the instrumentals, Brian Johnson helped them complete the lyrics. The week Bon Scott died, he'd gone down to the studio where they were working to lay down some drums while the Youngs worked out the guitar parts and he was going to start writing lyrics in earnest the (in what would be the week after his death). The last track Scott had laid some drums down on was for 'Let Me Put My Love Into You' which is one of *Back In Black*'s lesser known songs.

The band again hooked up with producer Mutt Lange but little did they all know just how successful *Back In Black* would become. Lange had a different approach to production than George Young who had produced all the band's albums up to but not including 1979's *Highway To Hell*. George was interested in energy, speed and rawness whereas Lange was all about structure, tone and melody. Lange is famously meticulous in his work and knows how to get the best out of a band, as evidenced now by his mighty body of work with Bryan Adams, The Cars, Def Leppard and Foreigner. Likewise AC/DC knew what they did best – they could not lose their rawness or even dirtiness; it is their trademark sound.

"With guitar riffs, we always look for something that's a little bit special," Angus once told *Guitar World*'s Jeff Gilbert in 1991. "We've always found that it is harder to come up with something that's nice and simple without getting something that's hard but easy. And a lot of it has to do with rhythm. We tend to go for, if we can, a bit more blues, a more rhythmic thing. Our riffs transport you. We don't know where, though."

British-born Tony Platt (who had worked with the band on *Highway To Hell*) engineered the album. It wasn't an easy album to make; the band had trouble right from the start and not just with the death of Bon Scott. With Brian Johnson in the band and a studio booked in the Bahamas, the band's equipment was held up at customs and the island was hit by severe tropical storms which Johnson makes reference to at the start of 'Hells Bells'. The weather hit the studio's electricity supply and slowed the band down while Johnson – who comes from the grainy North East of England – struggled to get to grips with the excessive temperament of the weather.

Cliff Williams went on to speak about the way the band record. "We've always recorded live, playing all four of us, together," he said to one interviewer at *Hard Rock Magazine* in1996. "As time's gone by, we tried to record with a click but … it's totally useless. We record basic tracks, track's bones, then Angus adds his guitar parts." The Youngs would typically have lots of riffs recorded as demos which Williams would listen to. Sometimes they'd have a notion about what they wanted out of Williams; the kind of bass-lines that worked best for their riffs. He would take this idea and add his own flare or perhaps sometimes just keep to their original idea.

Would the album have been different had Bon Scott been alive? Yes, but perhaps only slightly in terms of the musical back-drop, as the band had already laid down the bulk of the tracks before they hit the studio proper.

Back In Black opens with the pulsating 'Hells Bells' before they launch into the fast rocker 'Shoot To Thrill'. 'What Do You Do For Money Honey' is AC/DC at their cheekiest and the melody really makes this song work. 'Givin' The Dog A Bone' continues the band's jaunt into sexual innuendos while the same can be said for 'Let Me Put My Love Into You', which has an understated melody and some excellent backing vocals. The title track is undoubtedly one of the most profound examples of rock riffage at its best. 'You Shook Me All Night Long' is a rock song of mighty proportions and 'Have A Drink On Me' and 'Shake A Leg' are strong mid-paced rockers with plenty of gusto and charisma, while the closing track, 'Rock And Roll Ain't Noise Pollution', is a steady yet powerful salute to rock 'n' roll and what better band to say such words than AC/DC?

There is little to be said about *Back In Black* that hasn't been said before. Some claim *Highway To Hell* to be the band's finest effort; however *Back In Black* is by far the band's most successful release commercially and it proves they could not have made a better choice hiring singer Brian Johnson. His vocal style is less gritty and high-pitched than Bon Scott's and there's a stronger harmonic charm to his voice too. What Mutt Lange was adept at doing was harnessing the band's strength as a taut five-man unit. He knew that the band's strengths lay in creating mid-paced but hard stomping blues-tinged rockers and he gave them more room for melody. AC/DC's best tracks have always been the ones with firm stomp rather than a fast walk hence the success of this album (where aside from say, the lead riff to 'Shoot To Thrill', all the tracks are mid-paced). The production values are exquisite and Brian Johnson's voice is perfectly matched to the relentless blues-soaked riffage of Malcolm and Angus Young. Superficially there seems to be less bass on *Back In Black* than *Highway To Hell* but Williams' bold bass playing is the finest accompaniment to Phil Rudd's deceptively adept, understated drumming style.

Back In Black has aged remarkably well after thirty years. There isn't a bad track on this album and although some songs are less popular than others, AC/DC fans agree that it is such an important album because it opened up their fanbase considerably and, suddenly, they were popular not just with rock fans the world over but those music fans that wouldn't normally pick up an album with song titles like 'Hells Bells'. With *Back In Black*, AC/DC had now become a fully-fledged arena-headlining rock band.

Back In Black was released on July 25, 1980, just five months after the sad and untimely death of Bon Scott. It peaked at Number 1 in the UK and at a career-high of Number 4 in the USA; it eventually stayed in the *Billboard* 200 album charts for over 131 weeks. It was certified Platinum just three months after its release. It fared well in other countries too: it hit Number 1 in Australia, Canada and France; Number 6 in Austria; Number 8 in Norway; Number 12 in Sweden; Number 24 in New Zealand; Number 36 in Switzerland and Number 42 in Germany. *Back In*

AC/DC

Black's commercial strength – like Meat Loaf's *Bat Out Of Hell* – is in its longevity and the high quality of the songs that have made them popular outside of their usual fanbase.

The band have had higher charting albums such as 1981's *For Those About To Rock We Salute You* which hit Number 1 in the USA making it AC/DC's first Number 1 across the Atlantic and 2008's *Black Ice* which peaked at Number 1 in several countries. Chart positions do not necessarily mean high sales. Some albums could hit Number 1 yet drop out of the charts in weeks but some albums could have modest chart positions yet linger in the charts for years. Future albums *For Those About To Rock We Salute You* and *Black Ice* both sold millions but despite having a higher chart position than *Back In Black*, the band will perhaps never have a more successful album than that first one with Brian Johnson. *Back In Black* contains some of the band's most indelible songs, including 'You Shook Me All Night Long', 'Hells Bells', 'Shoot To Thrill' and the utterly magnetic, groove-laden title track. The album's biggest single was 'Rock And Roll Ain't Noise Pollution' which peaked at Number 15 in the UK Top 40 singles chart. The album also spawned 'You Shook Me All Night Long' as a single which peaked at Number 35 in the American *Billboard* list and Number 38 in the UK Top 40 singles chart. The stomping title track 'Back In Black' hit Number 37 in the American *Billboard* Hot 100 and Number 51 in the American *Billboard* Top Tracks chart. Meanwhile, 'Hells Bells' had peaked at Number 52 in the *Billboard* Top Tracks chart and 'Shoot To Thrill' peaked at Number 60 in said chart.

The plain yet striking all black album cover showed that the band were still in mourning after the accidental and tragic death of Bon Scott. Black is associated with funerals and death in the Western World and the band wanted to show that they were still grieving. Atlantic Records, however, were not initially bowled over by the stark album art and so the band allowed just a grey outline to be put around their bold logo.

The band filmed several videos to promote the album, shot in Breda in the Netherlands. The band captured videos for 'Back In Black', 'Hells Bells', 'What Do You Do For Money Honey',

'You Shook Me All Night Long', 'Let Me Put My Love Into You' and 'Rock And Roll Ain't Noise Pollution' (several of which were not released until 2005's video archive collection *Family Jewels* saw the light of day). The band actually remade the video for 'You Shook Me All Night Long' for 1986's *Who Made Who*, which was essentially the soundtrack for the Stephen King-directed film *Maximum Overdrive* (it too features on *Family Jewels*). The original video for the song had been released on *Back In Black: The Videos* but finally resurfaced in the 2009 box-set *Backtracks*. There is a difference between the 1980 video for 'You Shook Me All Night Long' and the 1986 version and not just with the concept: the former video features Phil Rudd who played drums on the original studio track while the latter version features the band's then-drummer Simon Wright who would later replace Rudd.

Singer Jess Cox of the Newcastle NWOBHM band Tygers Of Pan Tang told the author what he remembers about this transitional period in AC/DC's history: "I was then in this up-and-coming rock act who other kids were now getting into rock through – as I did – with AC/DC. I was even asked to comment on Bon's death in various national papers. All very surreal going from nobody in a bedroom to a rock star in eighteen months, never thinking anyone would be interested in my opinion on anything, ever. The following year they replaced Bon with Brian Johnson, a local guy known to us as he played in Geordie here in Newcastle. I guess AC/DC slipped off my radar too by then as it was right in the middle of the now burgeoning NWOBHM scene of which we were very much at the forefront of, so I had more to occupy my mind. But, then out came this new album with Brian singing on. I was absolutely floored by it. God what an opening, [the title track] 'Back In Black', the church funeral bell, the title, the mesmerising riff were all to me a tribute to Bon, laying his ghost and then the crunch of the main riff as it cranked up was like... and here is the new beginning. That album was just fantastic. Angus Young was just at his best. It was perfect and showed us upstart new kids how high we had to aim to compete.

AC/DC

"As a foot note I met Brian around this time. Somehow we were put together one night for a game of pool and he arrived in a four-wheel drive… Then they were top cock of the North. I certainly parked my white Montego Ariel out of sight round the corner that night. Anyway back to the story. [There appear to be numerous factors aligning Brian with the role as AC/DC frontman.] Brian [has] said he got the job through some fan suggesting they sign him as he sounded like Bon and was the same size as the band (they were not known for their height.) He also said he went into the audition and said: 'All reet lads, der ya fancy a singsong like,' in his best Geordie accent. He was on top form that night telling how his last gig before joining AC/DC was in some North East Working Man's club playing between the bingo and meat raffle draw and his next gig was the Houston Astrodome with AC/DC! Yikes! Not much difference there then. After the gig he was given the keys to a brand new Mercedes to run around in as he had no car! Couldn't happen to a nicer bloke. What was the question? Was I and the NWOBHM influenced by AC/DC? Just a bit…"

The album, however, did not go without its share of controversy when in 1985 the Parents Resource Music Centre listed 'Let Me Put My Love Into You' at Number 6 in their 'Filthy Fifteen' list of songs that they felt would be a negative influence on the youth of America.

Reviews of the band's first album with Brian Johnson were, on the whole, very positive. *Rolling Stone*'s revered rock writer David Fricke wrote in 1980: "*Back In Black* is not only the best of AC/DC's six American albums, it's the apex of heavy metal art: the first LP since *Led Zeppelin II* that captures all the blood, sweat and arrogance of the genre. In other words, *Back In Black* kicks like a mutha."

Writer and revered critic Robert Christgau gave *Back In Black* a B- in his famed *Consumer Guide Reviews* back in 1980 and wrote: "Replacing Aerosmith as primitives of choice among admirers of heavy machinery, these Aussies are a little too archetypal for my tastes. Angus Young does come up with killer riffs, though not as consistently as a refined person like myself might hope, and fresh recruit Brian Johnson sings like there's a cattle prod at his scrotum, just the thing for fans who can't decide whether their newfound testosterone is agony or ecstasy."

Some critics have commented that the band's lyrical output post-Bon Scott was very similar to what was written during 1974-1979; well, that's because the Young brothers had been writing lyrics together since they were teenagers, long before they'd met Scott. Similarly to ZZ Top, AC/DC's lyrics are often humorous, filled with innuendos and cheeky references to sex with no mention of politics or religion. Such criticisms were made in *Sounds* back in 1980 as respected journalist Phil Sutcliffe told the author of this book in 2010 when asked what it was like interviewing the band during the 1970s: "Loads of fun. I just liked every one of them hugely and although I'm completely different in character to them, much quieter and not lairy at all, I think we recognised a straightforwardness in each other and we got on very well and did a couple of ace interviews for *Sounds*, full of fun and great stories but also getting down to some engaging truths about their nature I think. Shame we never talked again after they fell out with me over my *Sounds* review of *Back In Black* (because I adversely compared Brian's lyrics with Bon's) but I entirely understood that even back then – it was a sensitive matter and I was being the critic, saying what I felt, and that was naturally intolerable to them at the time."

Since the album's original 1980 release, it has continued to receive adulation and acclaim from all corners of the music press worldwide, while its legacy as one of the greatest hard rock albums of all-time remains undiminished. It's amazing (or perhaps not, depending on your point of view) how this album has grown in stature over the years. It has won so many awards and tops so many polls and lists that AC/DC could quite easily sit back and live off the royalties from this one album alone but there is a thirst and hunger in the band that always drives them to create more mind-blowing music.

Black In Black has become not only AC/DC's most successful album but one of the most popular albums of all-time. It is a flawless rock release that has shifted over twenty million copies in the USA alone and 49 million worldwide. It is one of the top five best-selling albums in the USA along with *Thriller* by Michael Jackson, The Eagles' *Greatest Hits 1971-1975* and Led Zeppelin's *Led Zeppelin IV* and has earned over twenty Platinum records in the States. *Back In Black* is also one of the top three best-selling albums of all-time worldwide and the biggest selling album released by an Australian act. The only albums reported to have sold more copies worldwide than *Back In Black* are said to be Jackson's album and Pink Floyd's progressive rock masterpiece *The Dark Side Of The Moon*.

"I get amazed a bit sometimes when you see a lot of young bands who've come up from tough parts of town, especially the rap guys," said Malcolm Young to Tim Henderson of *BW&BK* in 2000. "You see them just buying everything straight away and then six months later they've no more hits, no more money. 'Scots are thrifty!', you know. We're not tight, but we do know what the value of a dollar is." The various reissues of *Back In Black* (the 1994 reissue, the 1997 *Bonfire* box-set reissue; the 2003 reissue and the 2004 Dueldisc reissue) have kept sales ticking over nicely.

"I've always been one for the simple things," Angus later confessed to Paul Cashmere of *Undercover* in 2008. "I have never been one for the flashy lifestyle. I think that is the same for everyone in AC/DC. I think that is why we stand out as who we are. We are just one of those bands. I think if you said to someone to describe you a rock guitarist they wouldn't picture somebody like myself, with the shorts and the school suit on. I think we have always been different from the rest."

Back In Black has been listed in far too many polls to name here but suffice to say the album is generally regarded as a milestone in the hard rock genre whilst it has also brought a lot of newcomers to the scene. *Rolling Stone* rated it Number 26 in their poll of the '100 Greatest Albums Of The '80s' and named the title track as one of the '500 Greatest Songs Of All-Time'. *Rolling Stone* love the album so much they also listed it in their 2003 poll of the '500 Greatest Albums Of All-Time'. The UK magazine *Q* named it one of the '40 Best Albums Of The '80s' in

2006 and *Back In Black* has also been named one of the '100 Best Australian Albums'.

However, even with the success of *Back In Black,* would they be able to retain their famously loyal fanbase? Maybe they'd lose a few fans but gain some more? Bon Scott biographer Clinton Walker told the author in 2009: "I first saw AC/DC at Festival Hall in Brisbane in about 1974 or 1975 and quite liked them, saw them a couple more times, they were sort of glam but also hard rock and I liked that, but then punk sort of swept them away but then I quickly came back to them, but I have to say … I kind of really lost interest after Bon died."

The band launched the mammoth *Back In Black* Tour in Belgium at the end of June in 1980 and finished touring the world in Australia in February, 1981. The set-list celebrated not only the strength of the new album but also the Bon Scott material. Opening with 'Hells Bells', they blitzed through 'Shot Down In Flames', 'Sin City', 'Back In Black', 'Bad Boy Boogie', 'The Jack', 'Highway To Hell', 'What Do You Do For Money Honey', 'High Voltage', 'Shoot To Thrill', 'Whole Lotta Rosie', 'You Shook Me All Night Long' and 'T.N.T.' before ending with 'Let There Be Rock'.

Rock writer Rob Evans caught the band at the Deeside Leisure Centre in Queensferry on November 6, 1979. He remembers: "The death of Bon Scott a mere four months later has been well-documented in many a tome, but what arrived next surprised many, including myself. With a gap of only three months from the date of Bon's untimely death the band released their epochal album *Back In Black* and started their world tour in, of all places, Belgium a month later. With Brian Johnson firmly ensconced into the AC/DC fold, I got my first taste of the new line-up when they rolled up to the Deeside Leisure Centre in Queensferry, Wales – and not Liverpool, as it is often geographically quoted – exactly a year to the day since I saw them at the Empire. An ice rink by day, the Leisure Centre was a cavernous and cold cow-shed of a building that could quite easily accommodate four to five thousand people and tonight it was packed. If truth be told I hated the venue when it was this

Bon's successor Brian Johnson with Angus onstage in Toronto, December 1981.
Courtesy of TB/TS/Keystone USA/Rex Features

busy. The view was limited, it was cold on the feet and it wasn't the easiest of places to get to. But with 'DC on the kind of form that they were it didn't take long for them to warm this venue up and truth be told we were lucky not to be standing in a foot of water, with steam rising as the ice was well and truly melted by this blistering performance. Brian Johnson had slipped into the fold well and new tracks like 'Hells Bells', 'Back In Black', 'You Shook Me All Night Long' and 'What Do You Do For Money Honey' all dovetailed perfectly with the more established tracks on offer. A rousing finish of 'T.N.T' and 'Let There Be Rock' sent this partisan crowd home on a high. I only ever managed to catch them live a few more times after this and as good as they were they never matched the display seen at both Liverpool and Deeside. Whilst I appreciated the Johnson years, it was always the Scott-era that showed this band in their true light. They were simple yet effective, but with a real sense of humour."

AC/DC went on to headline the second Monsters Of Rock Festival at Castle Donington in England on August 22, 1981 with a typically super-powered performance. Even so, some fans were critical. "I didn't go on the *Back In Black* tour, partially because the prices went up and I was a poor student with limited funds, which went on seeing bands that were lighter and less mainstream," says rock writer Phil Ashcroft of *Fireworks* magazine to the author. "I was also appalled that they'd carried on without missing a beat after losing the main man. I even left Donington before they played, but of course hindsight proves that their biggest success was yet to come."

Asked by Sylvie Simmons of *Creem* in 1982 if he had become a sex symbol since he shot to fame as AC/DC's frontman, Brian Johnson modestly replied: "Who me? You're joking, a sex symbol? Och! Thing is though, these gigs in America, the boys were sitting around in the dressing-room last week and saying, 'Do you know this is the first time we've actually had girls scream?' In Europe it's nearly all lads, but since we started this tour there's been a lot of girls. I don't know. I think it's because we're on the fooking radio so much. It can't be me good looks."

AC/DC

AC/DC had become one of the biggest stadium rock acts in the world but they were still not necessarily the most well-known. None of them were celebrities like Freddie Mercury of Queen or Steve Tyler of Aerosmith but this was deliberate, a consequence of the fact they led such a low-key life off-stage. "It has a life of its own and fans expect me to wear it 24-hours a day but as you can see, I don't," commented Angus when asked about his school uniform during an interview with Jacqui Swift of *The Sun* in 2008. "The advantage of it, though, is that I can walk down the street and not be mobbed as people don't recognise me. They are looking for somebody in a school suit."

When Bon Scott was alive, AC/DC had almost reached the top but after his death they exceeded all expectations and in a sadly ironic way, *Back In Black* had made it possible.

POSTSCRIPT

POSTHUMOUS RELEASES –
IN MEMORY OF BON SCOTT

"He [Bon] had a lot of acquaintances but not too many real close friends."

**Mark Evans speaking to the author
for *Rocktopia* in 2012**

1980 saw various single reissues featuring Bon Scott: 'Whole Lotta Rosie' from *If You Want Blood (You've Got It)* which reached Number 36 in the UK charts; 'Dirty Deeds Done Dirt Cheap' from the album of the same name which hit Number 47 in the UK; 'High Voltage' from the album of said title which reached Number 48 and also Bon Scott's iconic 'It's A Long Way To The Top (If You Wanna Rock 'N' Roll)', which peaked at Number 55 in the UK Top 40 singles chart (All singles aside from 'Whole Lotta Rosie' were part of a set of re-issues that included Saxon, Montrose and others; all released on the same day due to the fact that all of sudden metal singles were selling – would they have happened anyway even with Scott still in the band?). Also in 1980, the French band Trust penned the song 'Ton Dernier Acte' in memory and tribute to Bon Scott. Then as a reminder of the Bon Scott-era line-up, September 1981 saw the theatrical release of *Let There Be Rock: The Movie – Live In Paris,* which had been filmed at the revered Pavillon De Paris, France on December 9, 1979.

In terms of further posthumous releases, AC/DC have brought out several products featuring Bon Scott since his death. As a tribute, the band issued *'74 Jailbreak* in 1984 which contains five tracks: 'Jailbreak', 'You Ain't Got A Hold On Me', 'Show Business', 'Soul Stripper' and 'Baby, Please Don't Go'.

Fast forward to 1997 and AC/DC issued the commemorative box-set *Bonfire*, which features the live albums *Live From The Atlantic Studios* and *Let There Be Rock: The Movie – Live In Paris.* Both releases had previously been heavily bootlegged by fans. It also included *Back In Black* which was a tribute to Bon Scott and a rarities album with out-takes and live cuts. The box-set came under fire from serious enthusiasts for a lack of new material but the band honestly explained that they did not have a secret vault containing dozens of previously unreleased Bon Scott-sung material. The exhaustive archive box-set *Backtracks* was released in 2009 and contains some Bon Scott rarities as does the 2005 DVD *Family Jewels* and the 2007 box-set *Plug Me In*. George Young and Harry Vanda helped them select the tracks which brought back a lot of memories for the band.

In 2011, the aforementioned legendary concert film *Let There Be Rock* was finally released on DVD to rave reviews from fans and critics. The track-listing runs as follows: 'Live Wire', 'Shot Down In Flames', 'Hell Ain't A Bad Place To Be', 'Sin City', 'Walk All Over You', 'Bad Boy Boogie', 'The Jack', 'Highway To Hell', 'Girls Got Rhythm', 'High Voltage', 'Whole Lotta Rosie', 'Rocker' and 'Let There Be Rock'. The CD version actually features 'T.N.T.' after 'Rocker'. As the list suggests, the concert offers a mouth-watering collection of songs; some of the best tracks Bon Scott recorded with AC/DC.

Author Anthony Bozza who penned the sleeve notes for the DVD told *Classic Rock Revisited*'s Jeb Wright in 2011: "The box-set is great for younger fans that never got to see Bon with the band. There are a lot of people who may not even realise that AC/DC had two singers because Brian Johnson performs a lot

A statue honouring Bon Scott, in Fremantle, Western Australia.
Courtesy of Philip Hill/Rex Features

of Bon's material." AC/DC was a like an unstoppable machine back in the 1970s. The purpose of these reissues and tributes is not only to remember how great Bon Scott was, but for the younger fans to understand and acknowledge that there was another singer in the band before Brian Johnson.

A genuine legend in Australia and around the world, many other tributes have been paid to Bon Scott: in 2003 AC/DC and Bon Scott were inducted into the Rock And Roll Hall Of Fame and members of Scott's family attended the ceremony and even joined the band onstage to accept the honour in his memory. In May 2006, Bon Scott's original hometown of Kirriemuir in Scotland held a service in his memory and unveiled a stone slab in tribute. A message written by his long-term mate and member of The Valentines Vince Lovegrove was read aloud. Further tributes in his memory continued with a street in Kirriemuir being named after him and a bronze statue at Fremantle Fishing Boat Harbour in Western Australia being unveiled on February 24, 2008.

During promotional work for his autobiography, *Dirty Deeds: My Life Inside/Outside Of AC/DC*, former bassist Mark Evans spoke about Bon Scott's possible plans for a solo album. "When we started talking about it, it was probably about 5a.m. in the morning. The way he was speaking to me about it [it sounded like] in his own mind he knew a few guys that he wanted to play on it and I know that he had a couple of studios in mind and all that. I guess it would have made for a very interesting band. When he brought it up you don't know what the future would have held if he'd been around. It was something he wanted to do. He was very much into those bands like Little Feet, Lynyrd Skynyrd, and Allman Brothers-type stuff. He really liked that stuff. It was goin' to be something like that crossed with Little Richard, I guess. There were certainly no concrete plans to do anything about it. He wasn't being whimsical about it. It was certainly something he wanted to do if time would have allowed it. It would have been great but it was one of those things that never happened."

As with any singer or public figure that dies young, they receive almost mythic status in death and Bon Scott has become one of the most iconic frontmen in rock with the likes of Freddie Mercury of Queen and Phil Lynott of Thin Lizzy. He's a hero to many and an icon to most. The creative output from AC/DC during 1973 to 1980 was flawed but with time it has aged remarkably well and even thirty years later AC/DC's live set-lists still heavily feature songs from that period of their career. In 2004, *Classic Rock* magazine rated Bon Scott the Number 1 band leader in their '100 Greatest Frontmen Of All-Time' poll even beating Freddie Mercury of Queen and Led Zeppelin's Robert Plant. In 2006, *Hit Parader* placed Scott in the Number 5 position in their list of '100 Greatest Heavy Metal Vocalists Of All-Time'. In March 2012 a film based on Bon Scott's life called *Bon Scott: The Legend OF AC/DC* went into pre-production. The film, which is scripted by Rob Liotti of the covers band T.N.T., focuses on the time-frame between the band's breakthrough and Bon's untimely death. The film is backed by the US company High Voltage Productions. Such a film could bring Bon's name to a whole new generation of fans.

The band have continued to pay their respects to Bon Scott and have done it with dignity and pride and Bon Scott's replacement – Brian Johnson – has graciously expressed his admiration for the singer. Johnson refuses to sing the classic 'It's A Long Way To The Top (If You Wanna Rock 'N' Roll)' out of respect for his predecessor. It was his song.

Over the years Bon Scott's name has grown in stature more than even he would ever have imagined.

The legend lives on. RIP Bon Scott.

AFTERWORD I
BY
BRUCE KULICK
(GRAND FUNK RAILROAD)

To me, AC/DC represents the ultimate guitar-based riff rock that leaves the listener playing air guitar, moving wildly in sync with some of the best played anthems of our time.

Powerful guitar riffs from the Angus brothers truly define this band, but that sound was equally matched by a voice unique in conviction, delivered in spades by Mr Bon Scott.

Add in the thundering drum beats and pumping bass-lines from a formidable rhythm section and you have a perfect storm of rock music that created the best in guitar-based rock 'n' roll.

Take the song, 'Highway To Hell', heard around the world millions of times. The catchy lyrics and chord changes truly show the unique appeal of this band.

From sold-out stadiums and arenas everywhere, or even your local cinema, AC/DC's music appears boldly and without mistake, as a 'take no prisoners' approach to rock.

Bruce Kulick
www.kulick.net

AFTERWORD II
BY
DORO

Bon Scott was the most charismatic, soulful, powerful rock singer that ever lived. His awesome personality and his amazing voice were both one of a kind and still, to this day, are an inspiration for millions of people, rock fans and rock musicians worldwide.

I still remember the day when I heard him sing for the first time back in the mid-1970s when I was ten or eleven-years-old and I knew I'd never ever forget that feeling. I got chills like I'd never gotten before and I was totally hooked.

To me AC/DC with Bon Scott was an eye-opening, mind-blowing experience and I still love his music, his cool vibe, his sound and his songwriting.

Highway To Hell was a milestone in rock music and Bon is, and will forever be, a true legend. His heart always shined through and made people feel great and we all know he will be unbeatable, unforgettable and truly loved for all times.

God bless you, Bon!

Doro Pesch
www.doropesch.com

PART II: THE AFTERMATH

APPENDIX I

FOR THOSE ABOUT
TO ROCK – THE BRIAN
JOHNSON YEARS

Although this book is about the early years of AC/DC, to truly understand the impact of the Bon Scott era, it's worth giving a chronology of albums and important events after Scott's untimely death in February, 1980. The band's working ethic and style of music has changed very little since the early years as detailed in this book. The author has also chosen to offer some final thoughts on AC/DC as they stand in 2012 and how things have changed so dramatically for them since the band was formed in November 1973.

Following on from *Back In Black,* the band again hooked up with Mutt Lange for the last time for 1981's *For Those About To Rock We Salute You*, which was a commercial hit but not quite as highly lauded by the critics as its two predecessors were in 1979 and 1980. The now iconic title is a pun on the history book, *For Those About To Die We Salute You* by Robert Graves. The title track 'For Those About To Rock (We Salute You)' has become a must-play live song.

However, the follow-up to *Back In Black* did get some good reviews, noticeably one in *Rolling Stone* by the esteemed rock wordsmith Kurt Loder: "On *For Those About to Rock We Salute You*,

AC/DC

AC/DC's best album, the case for the band's talents is finally made with undeniable force and clarity. You want anthems? Here, they abound, from the title track's avalanche attack – complete with booming cannonades, of course – to 'Night Of The Long Knives', a rousing singalong reminiscent of the classic mid-1960s Anglo-pop tradition."

The band then underwent something of a critical decline in the 1980s though they did not do too bad commercially with *For Those About To Rock* (1981; Number 3 in the UK charts), *Flick Of The Switch* (1983; Number 3), *Fly On The Wall* (1985; Number 7), the compilation soundtrack *Who Made Who* (1986; Number 11) and *Blow Up Your Video* (1988; Number 2) although they would remain a top draw on the live stage. Would they ever reach the critical success of *Highway To Hell* or *Back In Black* again? It seemed unlikely back in the 1980s.

Reviews were not especially great for any of those albums. "Produced by the band, *Flick Of The Switch* isn't quite the monster blowout that 1980's *Back In Black* was," David Fricke wrote in *Rolling Stone* in 1983, "and the Young's retooling of old riffs for new hits also teeters on self-plagiarism at times."

"Angus Young is also in great form," wrote Tim Holmes of the album *Fly On The Wall* in *Rolling Stone* circa 1985, "playing the dumbest, most irresistibly repetitive chords in the lexicon."

Writing about *Who Made Who* in the mid-1980s, Robert Christgau said in his authoritative *Consumer Guide Reviews*: "I wish their only great work of art, the drum-hooked fucksong (sic) 'You Shook Me All Night Long', wasn't buried on side one the way it's buried in *Black In Black*. But this is their most presentable collection nevertheless."

The revered Robert Christgau also wrote in his *Consumer Guide Reviews* of 1988's *Blow Up Your Video*: "Their reunion with Vanda & Young no more signals their renewed determination to make good albums than Elton John's reunion with Bernie Taupin. It signals commercial panic, and unlike Elton they're unlikely to reverse their downward sales path over the long haul."

It appeared to some that AC/DC had lost their spark in the studio; sure, on stage, they were still an incredible band but the ideas didn't come out of the studio they way they used to. They needed somebody as intensive and strong-headed as Mutt Lange to steer them toward the right direction again. Mutt Lange would give members of Def Leppard their demo tapes to listen to in their cars while they were driving because that's how the music would sound on radio. Perhaps AC/DC needed those ideas and challenges too?

Brian Johnson would be seen at every show wearing his trademark flat cap, which kept him close to his working-class North of England roots (though he had moved to Florida on a permanent basis). The cap was recommended to him by his brother Maurice who works for the band as a cook; his brother said he should wear the cap onstage to stop the sweat dripping down his face and into his eyes and mouth from his thick curly hair. Like Angus's schoolboy uniform, the flat cap became a part of the band's iconic if unusual imagery.

It wasn't until *The Razor's Edge* in 1990 that they would have a revival of fortunes after which they put out their first live album with Brian Johnson in 1992, simply called *Live*. 1995's *Ballbreaker* and 2000's *Stiff Upper Lip* were successful and mostly well-received by critics although some suggested that the band had slowed down and ideas were lacking. Reviews of said albums were significantly better than their post-*For Those About To Rock We Salute You* albums though there were still some complaints. Of *The Razor's Edge*, Greg Sandow wrote in *Entertainment Weekly* in 1990: "If you're a hard rock addict — if raucous rock 'n' roll intensity is what you want — this is one album that really delivers. [Score:] A-"

Notably, in 1994 Phil Rudd was back in the band (having left in 1983). "I love to play with Phil," Cliff Williams said to an interviewer at *Hard Rock Magazine* in 1996. The two drummers Simon Wright and Chris Slade took his place and were both first-class musicians; Simon Wright replaced Phil after *Flick Of The Switch*'s recording session and was himself replaced by Chris Slade. While being very respectful of these two very talented musicians, Chris Williams was also open about his love of playing alongside Rudd: 'There's just one Phil Rudd."

AC/DC

Writing about *Ballbreaker* sometime after its original release back in 1995, Stephen Thomas Erlewine said on *All Music Guide*: "What makes *Ballbreaker* different than the albums AC/DC churned out during the [19]80s is simple – it's a matter of focus. Although 'Hard As A Rock' comes close, there aren't any songs as immediately memorable as any of their [19]70s classics, or even 'Moneytalks'."

Stiff Upper Lip was greeted with mostly positive reviews. The band had encouraged George Young to come out of retirement because they wanted to get that back-to-basics blues sound which was previously missing from many of their 1980s and early 1990s albums. One reviewer wrote about *Stiff Upper Lip* in the *NME*: "There are no pretensions above, below or beyond that one single-minded, unashamed aim. To rock. Why the fuck would a rock band wanna do anything else? They never ask that question, by the way. They don't have to. They just do it and it is we, listening to the stunning simplicity of *Stiff Upper Lip*, who are moved to wonder why on earth anyone would be daft enough to aim for anything else."

The band have never veered away from the same formula. Certainly, the music with Brian Johnson isn't as fast as Bon Scott's material; it's mid-paced yet still authentically AC/DC. "Oh, there isn't any secret," the ever modest Brian Johnson once told Alan Di Perna of *Guitar World* in 2000. "When you're singing with AC/DC, it kind of comes natural. You get caught up in the enthusiasm of it all. Everybody's whackin' away 100 percent; if you don't join in, you may as well not be there. As Ang and Mal have always said, the voice can be like another instrument and contribute to the sound of the band. Rather than just being the guy in the front standing there like a big tart wiggling his hips."

Impressively, 2008's *Black Ice* became the band's most successful record both critically and commercially since 1980's *Back In Black*. There were rumours amongst fans that *Black Ice* would be a farewell album though the band have since hinted that they may record again. Speaking at the time of the album's release, respected rock journalist Malcolm Dome told the author in 2009: "Yes.

I've now heard the whole album, and it is superb. If this is farewell… what a way to go out. On top of their game!"

Indeed, the long wait had been worth it.

"We had a bit of a break and we didn't have a lot of pressure to put out a new album because Sony were putting out compilations and DVDs," Angus told *Guitar World*'s Alan Di Perna in 2009. "So we could afford to sit back and say we'll do another album when we think we've got all the goods."

The band hooked up with revered American producer Brendan O'Brien who realised rather quickly that Brian Johnson doesn't enjoy working in a studio the way he enjoys singing onstage. "I hate the headphones, I hate the microphone stand – I want the mic in my hand – I hate all the bits of wood around you and I hate the feeling that I'm the only f[uck]er there," the singer told Kathy McCabe of the Australian broadsheet, *Daily Telegraph* in 2011, "I came in and there was an old glassed-in office behind the reception desk and he put this mic in there, with a little mixing desk and two speakers and had his tech guy on the computer to start the tape."

Mike Fraser who mixed and engineered the album and had previously worked with the band on *The Razor's Edge*, *Ballbreaker* and *Stiff Upper Lip* told Tim Henderson at *BW&BK* in 2008: "They are never going to get back to that *Flick Of The Switch* or *High Voltage* sound, because they aren't the twenty-year-old kids anymore either. Your whole persona kind of changes. How do you write about getting laid and drunk every night if you're not doing it, if you know what I mean? (laughs) There are a lot of bands that have been around for a while, and I think they have a harder and harder time to stay street-connected with the kids, when you aren't really a kid yourself."

In terms of the band dynamics in the studio, Fraser told *Classic Rock*'s Geoff Barton in 2008: "There isn't really a leader in the band *per se*. Malcolm is definitely the anchor. He's probably one of the best rhythm guitar players I've ever worked with, as far as timing and groove and everything goes. It's just amazing. When AC/DC play live, most of the guys in the band watch Malcolm for all the cues and everything. Malcolm might look like he's in the background but all eyes are on him, for sure. In the studio it's a team effort, however."

Reviewers gushed over the band's latest opus when it was released in 2008. It is arguably one of their finest releases to date. Alexis Petridis wrote in *The Guardian*: "But *Black Ice* clearly isn't a record particularly interested in what the layman thinks: if you've sold 200 million albums worldwide, you don't really need to go around touting for new clients. It's a record aimed at the band's existing audience, and far more important than any qualitative highs and lows is the fact that everything you might expect is present and correct."

Writing in *The Village Voice*, Richard Bienstock said: "Producer Brendan O'Brien... not only restores the pristine vintage Marshall guitar sound – bright, warm, ever-so-slightly overdriven – of the band's classic [19]70s efforts with producers Harry Vanda and big brother George Young, but also lifts a key element of their mega-selling Mutt Lange–produced trilogy: gigantic, gang-vocal-soaked choruses."

A number of releases followed the success of *Black Ice*, which sold eight million copies worldwide and hit Number 1 in over a dozen countries. *Black Ice* was recorded and mixed at Bryan Adams' studio The Warehouse in Vancouver, Canada, and is also the band's most up-tempo release since *The Razor's Edge* almost twenty years before. Some of those releases included their second soundtrack compilation *Iron Man 2*; a mundane effort but good for casual fans. It sold millions after its release in 2010. And 2011's excellent DVD *Live At River Plate* proves that AC/DC are still an amazing live draw.

So that's it for the releases... but what will happen to the band in the future?

Albums from AC/DC are few and far between these days. There's no denying the fact that they still have something to say and can hold their own against any band regardless of age. AC/DC are a one-off band. At the time of writing, the band have spoken to the press about heading into the studio in late 2012 to record a new album set for release the following year, which would neatly coincide with their fortieth anniversary. However, speaking in January, Brian Johnson said recording of the album had been delayed. "One of the boys is a little sick and I can't say anything, but he's getting better," Johnson told the American radio programme, *The Cowhead Show* in 2012. "He's doing wonderful. Full recovery fully expected."

Despite the delay there's no question that the band wanted a new album recorded and set for a possible 2013/14 release. Johnson has even spoken about retirement albeit light-heartedly, saying that if he could no longer perform or sing good enough he'd want the guys in the band to tell him. Johnson would want them to find a suitable replacement so they could carry on the AC/DC name. For a man in his sixties he is in great shape; he is still a rock wailer!

AC/DC would never go onstage and commit themselves to year-long tours if they thought they were not up to it. Tours are incredibly demanding; there's not only the performances to think about but the constant travelling, rehearsals, soundchecks, interviews and such. It takes its toll. Some bands cannot hack it but AC/DC's *Black Ice* World Tour was a truly mouth-watering spectacle.

Outside of the band, each member has his own interests; Brian Johnson, for example, likes to build and race cars in his adopted home state, Florida. "I came from a mining village and nobody had any money," he told K.S. Wang of *Motor Trend* magazine in 2008. "I promised myself one day I would buy [a Rolls Royce Phantom]. It's the best car I've ever had."

Johnson stays grounded by travelling back to his native North East several times a year to visit family and friends; though he lives in Florida he is evidently proud of his Geordie roots. Angus, meanwhile, enjoys reading books on history, doesn't drink alcohol and prefers strong English tea and cigarettes and is married to a Dutch woman. Malcolm is a keen football fan and lives mostly in Sydney; Phil Rudd owns a farm, races cars and flies helicopters in New Zealand and Florida-based Cliff Williams enjoys fishing. They keep fit and healthy and it shows in their live performances. Like a lot of older, more experienced bands they tend not to hang out with each other when they're not working

AC/DC

on new music or touring together. The space apart helps fuel the enthusiasm for new projects.

"AC/DC is the best thing that ever happened to me," Cliff Williams told *Hard Rock* magazine in 1996, "so I hope of all my heart we'll continue. And [the] concerts are good, the kids have fun. We don't pretend to give something deep and intellectual. Just a good rock 'n' roll!"

In an age of celebrity rock stars and reality TV, AC/DC have shied away from publicity except around the time of an official release. They're not rock stars in an Aerosmith Steve Tyler sense; they a band that made it big and they get paid for doing something they love but they've managed to live low-key, low-profile lives and have shunned the press and mainstream exposure for much of their careers. Angus or Malcolm – two of the most influential guitarists in rock – could walk down any High Street and nobody would know it's them. They could walk past a young girl who's wearing an AC/DC t-shirt and she probably wouldn't realise she'd just walked past the creators of *Back In Black*. It's a comfortable and private life they have maintained for a long time now. And there's a certain class in that.

With time, their legacy has been re-appraised and certainly much of the press now cherishes them. During the 2003 release of the AC/DC remasters rock fans and critics who had originally snubbed the band for being unoriginal and pedestrian suddenly praised them for their longevity and uniqueness. It's almost as if their music had stayed dormant for years and had reappeared with a breath of fresh air and it just sounded different; somehow better. Of course, AC/DC had always been around; they may have slowed down their productivity yet they were still adored by millions around the world but their popularity appeared to have exploded in the noughties to heights not seen since the days of *Back In Black*. For reasons that cannot perhaps be described, their albums sound better now than ever before. Maybe that's to do with the decline and then slow re-emergence of rock after a decade spent out of fashion? Or maybe it's due to the legions of young rock bands that have paid their respects to AC/DC? After all, these guys know how to rock.

They were inducted into the Rock And Roll Hall Of Fame in 2003 and finally it seemed liked AC/DC were getting critical acceptance: they won their first Grammy in 2010 in the category of 'Best Hard Rock Performance' for 'War Machine' beating Metallica, Linkin Park, Alice In Chains and Nickelback.

In 2012, AC/DC can do little wrong. They're probably the biggest rock band in the world and fans still fondly remember the great Bon Scott. Who'd have thought such a thing would happen back in the mid-1970s when they were derided by critics? Their longevity is down to the simple and quite obvious fact that they have never changed what they do best. Their music is deceptively simple and raw and electric.

Speaking in 2007 to Mark Prindle of *Citizine*, the band's very first singer Dave Evans commented on AC/DC's longevity: "It's [Malcolm's] rhythm that everyone hears – that rhythm sound, that great sound, that's Malcolm Young. So no matter who's going to write songs with Malcolm, it's going to have Malcolm's sound, and so it's up to a singer to come up with choruses or lines and lyrics to go with Malcolm. So, really, it's been the same sound the whole time. And Brian's done a great job. Because he wouldn't have been there for so bloody long if he didn't do a good job! His record with the band speaks for itself."

However, the band still have their critics. Bon Scott biographer and Aussie rock writer Clinton Walker told the author of this book in 2009 when asked for his thoughts on *Black Ice* and the subsequent world tour: "Look, again, I've taken little interest; it sounds like much the same record they've been making for the past two decades. I'm not knocking it, AC/DC invented a whole thing kind of just like the Ramones did and so it's their liberty to just keep doing that thing forever more, but after a certain point I stopped listening to the Ramones and I've done the same with AC/DC."

Asked by the author if AC/DC are finally getting the reverence they deserve, AC/DC archivist and author Arnaud Durieux said during the time of the *Black Ice* World Tour in 2010: "Sure, not that they ever cared about being 'recognised' though. They certainly must enjoy the financial aspect of being enormous now, especially on this tour. Entirely deserved if you ask me!"

AC/DC's career has run parallel with many trends, including punk and the New Wave Of British Heavy Metal and yet somehow outlived them all. After what appeared to be the final wave of British bands invading American shores in the 1980s with the so-called "New Wave" made up of Duran Duran and The Cure *et al*, American rock bands started to emerge from colleges around the States, notably in Seattle which spawned the grunge scene (heavily influenced by punk and even metal). Of course, the Sunset Strip gave birth to the glam metal scene of the 1980s too with bands such as Mötley Crüe and Ratt. The point here is that those movements lasted only a short while; at some point, after however many years later, they ended. In the 1990s, when metal had been kicked in the arse by grunge and dropped out of the mainstream, alternative rock and metal bands such as Korn started to crop up. Yet AC/DC continued to do their own thing; much to the pleasure and even dismay of some rock fans.

"When the world was playing punk rock music, we were a rock 'n' roll band; when the world was playing disco music or whatever, we were a rock 'n' roll band," Angus told Brian Boyd of the UK's *Daily Telegraph* in 2008. "The only music principle we have is that when we record a song, we try to imagine that if it were to be played at a party then would it get people's feet tapping?"

Are AC/DC just a juvenile band? Well, wasn't rock 'n' roll originally created for kids? What are AC/DC supposed to sing about... the Mona Lisa? Charles Dickens, maybe? Nah, that's not their style.

The highbrow critics that had initially shunned them are now praising them; AC/DC are still here making music. Has their fanbase deserted them? No. They have their own demograph of fans: grandparents, parents and kids attend their shows. AC/DC are a rare band in that sense. Perhaps it is a tribute to their hard work over the years? Their fanbase continues to grow each year and *Black Ice* proved that they are more popular now than ever before. You go to an AC/DC gig and see a guy with a skinhead, tattoos and facial piercings but also a mature dude in casual clothes or a woman with a leather jacket and jeans. That is the beauty of this band. They transcend boundaries in many ways.

There are marked differences between the Bon Scott and Brian Johnson eras of the band, of course. Martin Popoff, the acclaimed Canadian metal author and historian, said to the author, "If I were to compare Brian Johnson and Bon Scott, first of all, love 'em both! Both eras of AC/DC have brought me much happiness in my life, in fact, probably more than any other band. But specifically, comparing the two singers, it's hard to separate them: one of them is pre-fame, bubbling under, and one of them is the front-charger of a huge stadium rock band. So in that sense, Bon always struck me as a punk rocker, the devilish input, the rabble-rouser, the David Lee Roth of the band; really, very much the leader, the guy who gets them into trouble. And it's also hard to forget that he was a little older than the other guys, with a little bit of embarrassing rock experience in his dark past ... I actually think the way he looks doesn't match his voice at all. But what a voice!

"Brian, even in the early years, but definitely in the latter years, is definitely uncomfortable to listen to because it sounds like he's going to explode, that his vocal chords are just going to flap out of his mouth and hang there. Love the guy as a frontman, the way he looks, as a personality, the way he dresses, that cute little hat. Love that he's English, and again, that the guy had some rock 'n' roll past before he came into AC/DC. Actually it's cool that he's English with the other guys and their Scottish roots. And it's pretty cool that he comes into the band and they become massive, so right away, he doesn't feel like a guest, a third wheel, the new guy, he feels like he's a big part of their success. And then of course, he's been there for thirty years now, so over the course of those thirty years, it was pretty easy to see him as a leader as well, which is something you want from a frontman."

Popoff continues to explore the differences between the two eras of AC/DC as he told the author: "With respect to the quality of the albums, and which is best, which has the best batch of songs, it also is hard to gauge. Well, maybe it's not. Maybe if, like Status Quo, like Ramone's, AC/DC are a band who stick to a very tight range, after a while, you're bound to be grumbling about repetition, running out of ideas, which I definitely feel is the case with albums like *Fly On The Wall*, and the album I feel that is their worst, *Blow Up Your Video*. It's true, the only album that I would put in my Top 4 even, from the Brian Johnson era, is *Flick Of The Switch*, which I love because it's just so heavy and raw and relentless. Really, it's hard to even rank *Back In Black* because it has so much massive baggage with it, but I do distinctly remember not liking it as much as *Highway To Hell* when it came out, and definitely the next one being a disappointment, a lackadaisical, second rate version of *Back In Black*, is *For Those About To Rock*. So yeah, it's hard to argue [against the idea] that their best material is with Bon. *But* again, the first two albums are definitely weak, *Let There Be Rock* just feels kind of cold, although I'll always have a fondness because it's the first AC/DC album I bought, and as a new release. No, my two favourite AC/DC albums are most definitely *Powerage* and *Highway To Hell*, the former for its laid-back, almost southern vibe, and the latter for that sterling bunch of really heavy songs all in a row, namely 'Walk All Over You', 'Touch Too Much' and 'Beating About The Bush'. The title track is pretty cool too, plus 'Girls Got Rhythm', heck, all of it is cool. It really is the most exciting, starry, sparkling of all the albums, because *Back In Black* is kind of dark and fuzzy and warm, as is the follow-up. I guess *Highway To Hell* is one of those what you would call a cusp album, where everything comes together, there's total magic, and it will never be the same again."

Asked by the author about the differences between the Bon Scott and Brian Johnson eras, Jake Brown – author of *AC/DC: In The Studio* – says, "I think they were building that brand of rock in the 1970s, and after solidifying it on *Highway To Hell*, they didn't want to rock the boat, so to speak, after they succeeded with *Back In Black* to transitioning that brand of hard rock successfully in the 1980s with a new singer and new decade, etc. Everything they made after *Back In Black* was essentially modelled on its musical fundamentals..."

AC/DC have become incredibly protective over their music, for years remaining arguably the biggest global act to not allow their back-catalogue to be sold on iTunes because in their opinion music fans are able to download individual songs which in effect destroys the power of the album. They have spent so long making their albums over a forty year period that they have adopted a purist approach to marketing and selling their music. As music sales decline AC/DC are still selling millions so they're obviously doing something right. The world is going digital but people are still buying AC/DC albums. Other artists could learn a thing or two from this band. They finally reversed this stance and released their back-catalogue (sixteen studio albums; over 150 million physical copies sold) digitally in the autumn of 2012. AC/DC's debut on iTunes sold 4800 digital albums and 696,000 songs.

At a time when pundits debate whether rock is dead given the rise in popularity of rap, R'N'B and disposable pop music plus the decline in CD sales, bands like AC/DC have fought for the cause. With songs to their name like 'Rock And Roll Ain't Noise Pollution' and 'Can't Stop Rock And Roll', AC/DC have spent the past forty years playing the music they love and never shying away from their true passion in life which is to play rock 'n' roll. It's been around since the days of Chuck Berry and pioneers like Ike Turner right through to the likes of the Rolling Stones in the 1960s, Deep Purple in the 1970s, Guns N' Roses in the 1980s, Green Day in the 1990s and the Foo Fighters in the 2000s. There are various styles in rock 'n' roll and a myriad of subgenres but AC/DC's roots are still based firmly in the blues style of playing.

Although Australians love to claim the band as their own, their music, image and naughty *Carry On*-style sense of humour is very British. The Young brothers have never shied away from their Scottish roots nor did the late Bon Scott – and Brian Johnson and Cliff Williams are both English – but in 2012 the band are spread all over the place. It's the power of rock music that brings them together despite the geographical distance.

In November 2012 AC/DC released *Live At River Plate* on CD following the huge success of the DVD. The terrific double CD

AC/DC

features not only some of the band's most well-known songs from the Brian Johnson era and an excellent choice of cuts from their recent album *Black Ice*, but also a healthy dose of Bon Scott-era numbers such as 'Hell Ain't A Bad Place To Be', 'Dirty Deeds Done Dirt Cheap', 'Shot Down In Flames', 'The Jack', 'Dog Eat Dog', 'T.N.T', 'Whole Lotta Rosie', 'Highway To Hell' and 'Let There Be Rock'. Such an amount of songs from the band's 1970s albums proves that the band's most creative and thrilling period was emphatically pre-1980. Those songs are not only fan favourites but genuine rock classics. Maybe Bon was looking down at the band as they played three mega shows in Buenos Aires in December 2009? He sure would have been proud. The band was on fire; simply stunning. AC/DC have now become a worldwide brand, a marketing force to be reckoned with but they are still at heart a straight-ahead rock 'n' roll band.

The band had always wanted to be true to themselves and their fans, as Angus told *Creem*'s Sylvie Simmons back in 1982: "I honestly don't think I could walk on that stage and do what I do or any of the lads do if we couldn't do it honest. If it all went bad, we would feel it more than anyone."

APPENDIX II
SELECTED
DISCOGRAPHY (UK)
(1973-1980)

The following discography details the UK only releases (unless otherwise stated) released by AC/DC between 1973 and Bon Scott's death in 1980 as well as any posthumous releases.

All releases feature Bon Scott in one way or another...

(NOTE: All track-listings correspond with current versions that are available on CD in the UK unless otherwise stated.)

ALBUMS
High Voltage: *Baby, Please Don't Go/She's Got Balls/Little Lover/Stick Around/Soul Stripper/You Ain't Got A Hold On Me/Love Song/Show Business*
LP – Albert 1975
NOTE: This was an Australian only release.

AC/DC

T.N.T.: *It's A Long Way To The Top (If You Wanna Rock 'N' Roll)/Rock 'N' Roll Singer/The Jack/Live Wire/T.N.T./Rocker/Can I Sit Next To You Girl/High Voltage/School Days*
LP – Albert 1975
NOTE: This was an Australian only release.

High Voltage: *It's A Long Way To The Top (If You Wanna Rock 'N' Roll)/Rock 'N' Roll Singer/The Jack/Live Wire/T.N.T./Can I Sit Next To You Girl/Little Lover/She's Got Balls/High Voltage*
LP – Atlantic 1976
NOTE: This was the band's first international release.

Dirty Deeds Done Dirt Cheap: *Dirty Deeds Done Dirt Cheap/Love At First Feel/Big Balls/Rocker/Problem Child/There's Gonna Be Some Rockin'/Ain't No Fun (Waiting Around To Be A Millionaire)/Ride On/Squealer*
LP – Atlantic 1976

Let There Be Rock: *Go Down/Dog Eat Dog/Let There Be Rock/Bad Boy Boogie/Problem Child/Overdose/Hell Ain't A Bad Place To Be/Whole Lotta Rosie*
LP – Atlantic 1977

Powerage: *Rock 'N' Roll Damnation/Down Payment Blues/Gimme A Bullet/Riff Raff/Sin City/What's Next To The Moon/Gone Shootin'/Up To My Neck In You/Kicked In The Teeth*
LP – Atlantic 1978

Highway To Hell: *Highway To Hell/Girls Got Rhythm/Walk All Over You/Touch Too Much/Beating Around The Bush/Shot Down In Flames/Get It Hot/If You Want Blood (You've Got It)/Love Hungry Man/Night Prowler*
LP – Atlantic 1979

LIVE ALBUMS

If You Want Blood You've Got It: *Riff Raff/Hell Ain't A Bad Place To Be/Bad Boy Boogie/The Jack/Problem Child/Whole Lotta Rosie/Rock 'N' Roll Damnation/High Voltage/Let There Be Rock/Rocker*
LP – Atlantic 1978

Live From The Atlantic Studios: *Live Wire/Problem Child/High Voltage/Hell Ain't A Bad Place To Be/Dog Eat Dog/The Jack/Whole Lotta Rosie/Rocker*
LP – Atlantic 1978
NOTE: *This was an official promo release and was later heavily bootlegged. It was released by the band officially in 1997 as part of the commemorative* Bonfire *box-set.*

Let There Be Rock: Then Movie – Live In Paris: *Live Wire/Shot Down In Flames/Hell Ain't A Bad Place To Be/Sin City/Walk All Over You//Bad Boy Boogie/The Jack/Highway To Hell/Girls Got Rhythm/High Voltage/Whole Lotta Rosie/Rocker/T.N.T./Let There Be Rock*
NOTE: *This was released by the band officially in 1997 as part of the commemorative* Bonfire *box-set.*

EPs

'74 Jailbreak: *Jailbreak/You Ain't Got A Hold On Me/Show Business/Soul Stripper/Baby, Please Don't Go*
CD – Atlantic 1984

AC/DC

SINGLES

Can I Sit Next To You Girl *(1974)*

Love Song (Oh Jene)/Baby, Please Don't Go *(1975)*
High Voltage *(1975)*
T.N.T. *(1976)*

It's A Long Way To The Top
(If You Wanna Rock 'N' Roll) *(1976)*
Jailbreak *(1976)*
Dirty Deeds Done Dirt Cheap *(1976)*

Dog Eat Dog *(1977)*
Love At First Feel *(1977)*
Let There Be Rock *(1977)*
Whole Lotta Rosie *(1977)*

Rock 'N' Roll Damnation *(1978)*
Whole Lotta Rosie *(Live) (1978)*

Girls Got Rhythm *(1979)*
Highway To Hell *(1979)*

Touch Too Much *(1980)*
Whole Lotta Rosie *(Live, reissue) (1980)*
Dirty Deeds Done Dirt Cheap *(Reissue) (1980)*
High Voltage *(Reissue) (1980)*
It's A Long Way To The Top
(If You Wanna Rock 'N' Roll) *(Reissue) (1980)*

Big Balls *(1981)*

Jailbreak *(1984)*

Dirty Eyes *(1997)*

BOX-SETS

Bonfire: *(Live From The Atlantic Studios)* Live Wire/Problem Child/High Voltage/Hell Ain't A Bad Place To Be/Dog Eat Dog/The Jack/Whole Lotta Rosie/Rocker *(Let There Be Rock: The Movie – Live In Paris)* Live Wire/Shot Down In Flames/Hell Ain't A Bad Place To Be/Sin City/Walk All Over You/Bad Boy Boogie/The Jack/Highway To Hell/Girls Got Rhythm/High Voltage/Whole Lotta Rosie/Rocker/T.N.T./Let There Be Rock *(Volts)* Dirty Eyes/Touch Too Much/If You Want Blood (You've Got It)/Back Seat Confidential/Get It Hot/Sin City/She's Got Balls/School Days/It's A Long Way To The Top (If You Wanna Rock 'N' Roll)/Ride On *(Back In Black)* Hells Bells/Shoot To Thrill/What Do You Want For Your Money Honey/Givin' The Dog A Bone/Let Me Put My Love Into You/Back In Black/You Shook Me All Night Long/Have A Drink On Me/Shake A Leg/Rock And Roll Ain't Noise Pollution
CD – East West 1997

Backtracks: *(Studio Rarities)* High Voltage/Stick Around/Love Song/It's A Long Way To The Top (If You Wanna Rock 'N' Roll)/Rocker/Fling Thing/Dirty Deeds Done Dirt Cheap/Ain't No Fun (Waiting Around To Be A Millionaire)/R.I.P. (Rock In Peace)/Carry Me Home/Crabsody In Blue/Cold Hearted Man/Who Made Me/Snake Eye/Borrowed Time/Down On The Borderline/Big Gun/Cyberspace *(Live Rarities)* Dirty Deeds Done Dirt Cheap/Dog Eat Dog/Shot Down In Flames/Back In Black/T.N.T./Let There Be Rock/Guns For Fire/Sin City/Rock And Roll Ain't Noise Pollution/This House Is On Fire/You Shook Me All Night Long/Jailbreak/Shoot To Thrill/Hell Ain't No Bad Place To Be *(Live Rarities)* High Voltage/Hells Bells/Whole Lotta Rosie/Dirty Deeds Done Dirt Cheap/Highway To Hell/Back In Black/For Those About To Rock/Ballbreaker/Hard As A Rock/Hail Caesar/Whole Lotta Rosie/You Shook Me All Night Long/Safe In New York City *(Family Jewels DVD)* Big Gun/Hard As A Rock/Hail

AC/DC

Caesar/Cover You In Oil/Stiff Upper Lip/Satellite Blues/Safe
In New York City/Rock 'N' Roll Train/Anything
Goes/Jailbreak/It's A Long Way To The Top (If You Wanna
Rock 'N' Roll)/Highway To Hell/You Shook Me All Night
Long/Guns For Hire/Dirty Deeds Done Dirt Cheap/Highway
To Hell *(Live At Circus Krone 2003)* Hell Ain't A Bad Place To
Be/Back In Black/Stiff Upper Lip/Shoot To
Thrill/Thunderstruck/Rock 'N' Roll Damnation/What's Next
To The Moon/Hard As A Rock/Bad Boy Boogie/The Jack/If
You Want Blood (You've Got It)/Hells Bells/Dirty Deeds Done
Dirt Cheap/Rock 'N' Roll Damnation/T.N.T./Let There Be
Rock/Highway To Hell/For Those About To Rock (We Salute
You)/Whole Lotta Rosie
CD/DVD – Columbia 2009
NOTE: The track-listing corresponds with the deluxe edition.

VHS/DVD
Let There Be Rock: The Movie – Live In Paris: Live
Wire/Shot Down In Flames/Hell Ain't A Bad Place To Be/Sin
City/Walk All Over You//Bad Boy Boogie/The Jack/Highway
To Hell/Girls Got Rhythm/High Voltage/Whole Lotta
Rosie/Rocker/Let There Be Rock
VHS – Warner Bros. 1980
DVD – Warner Bros. 2011

Family Jewels: *(Disc 1)* Baby, Please Don't Go/Show
Business/High Voltage/ It's A Long Way To The Top (If You
Wanna Rock 'N' Roll)/T.N.T./Jailbreak/Dirty Deeds Done
Dirt Cheap/Dog Eat Dog/Let There Be Rock/Rock 'N' Roll
Damnation/Sin City/Riff Raff/Fling Thing/Rocker/Whole
Lotta Rosie/Shot Down In Flames/Walk All Over You/Touch
Too Much/If You Want Blood (You've Got It)/Girls Got
Rhythm/Highway To Hell *(Disc 2)* Hells Bells/Back In
Black/What Do You Do For Money Honey/Rock And Roll
Ain't Noise Pollution/Let's Get It Up/For Those About To
Rock (We Salute You)/Flick Of The Switch/Nervous
Shakedown/Fly On The Wall/Danger/Sink The Pink/Stand

Up/Shake Your Foundations/Who Made You/You Shook Me All Night Long/Heatseeker/That's The Way I Wanna Rock 'N' Roll/Thunderstruck/Moneytalks/Are You Ready
DVD – Sony 2005

Plug Me In: *(Disc 1 – Bon Scott era)* High Voltage/It's A Long Way To The Top (If You Wanna Rock 'N' Roll)/School Days/T.N.T./Live Wire/Can I Sit Next To You Girl/Baby, Please Don't Go/Hell Ain't A Bad Place To Be/Rocker/Rock 'N' Roll Damnation/Dog Eat Dog/Let There Be Rock/Problem Child/Sin City/Bad Boy Boogie/Highway To Hell/The Jack/Whole Lotta Rosie *(Disc 2 – Brian Johnson era)* Shot Down In Flames/What Do You Do For Money Honey/You Shook Me All Night Long/Let There Be Rock/Back In Black/T.N.T./Shoot To Thrill/Guns For Hire/Dirty Deeds Done Dirt Cheap/Flick Of The Switch/Bedlam In Belgium/Back In Black/Highway To Hell/Whole Lotta Rosie/For Those About To Rock (We Salute You)/Gone Shootin'/Hail Caesar/Ballbreaker/Rock And Roll Ain't Noise Pollution/Hard As A Rock/Hells Bells/Ride On/Stiff Upper Lip/Thunderstruck/If You Want Blood (You've Got It)/The Jack/You Shook Me All Night Long *(Disc 3 – Between The Cracks)* She's Got Balls/It's A Long Way To The Top (If You Wanna Rock 'N' Roll)/Let There Be Rock/Bad Boy Boogie/Girls Got Rhythm/Guns For Hire/This House Is On Fire/Highway To Hell/Girls Got Rhythm/Let There Be Rock *(Disc 3 – Live At The Summit 1983)* Guns For Hire/Shoot To Thrill/Sin City/This House Is In Fire/Back In Black/Bad Boy Boogie/Rock And Roll Ain't Noise Pollution/Flick Of The Switch/Hells Bells
DVD – Sony 2007

AC/DC

MUSIC VIDEOS
High Voltage *(1975)*
Baby, Please Don't Go *(1975)*
Show Business *(1975)*

Jailbreak *(1976)*
It's A Long Way To The Top (If You Wanna Rock 'N' Roll)
(1976)
Problem Child *(1976)*
Baby, Please Don't Go *(1976)*
Dirty Deeds Done Dirt Cheap *(1976)*

Dog Eat Dog *(1977)*
Let There Be Rock *(1977)*

Rock 'N' Roll Damnation *(1978)*
Sin City *(1978)*
Riff Raff *(1978)*
Fling Thing/Rocker *(1978)*
Whole Lotta Rosie *(1978)*

Shot Down In Flames *(1979)*
Walk All Over You *(1979)*
Touch Too Much *(1979)*
If You Want Blood (You've Got It) *(1979)*

Girls Got Rhythm *(1980)*
Highway To Hell *(1980)*

NOTABLE TOURS

Australian Club Dates *(1974-1975)*
High Voltage Australian Tour *(1975)*
TNT/Lock Up Your Daughters Summer Vacation Tour *(1975-1976)*
High Voltage Tour/Lock Up You Daughters Tour *(1976)*
Dirty Deeds Done Dirt Cheap UK Tour/A Giant Dose Of Rock 'N' Roll Australian Tour *(1976-1977)*
Let There Be Rock Tour *(1977)*
Powerage Tour *(1978)*
If You Want Blood Tour *(1978-1979)*
Highway To Hell Tour *(1979)*

(NOTE: The official AC/DC website www.acdc.com details every AC/DC tour; for an in-depth and exhaustive history also visit the superb fan-site run by leading AC/DC expert Arnaud Durieux: www.ac-dc.net.)

APPENDIX III
SELECTED TIMELINE
1973-1980

Here are some important dates in the AC/DC timeline between 1973 and 1980:

(NOTE: Not all precise dates have been specified but where possible exact dates have been given.)

1973

November – AC/DC was formed in Sydney, New South Wales.

December 31 – AC/DC played at the popular Sydney nightclub, Chequers.

1974

February – Bassist Larry Van Kriedt left AC/DC and was later replaced by Rob Bailey after a brief spot by Neil Smith.

February – Drummer Colin Burgess left the band.

AC/DC

April – Drummer Peter Clack joined the band after brief spots by Ron Carpenter, Russell Coleman and Noel Taylor.

July 22 – The single 'Can I Sit Next To You, Girl' was released in Australia.

October 24 – Reportedly the date when Bon Scott joined AC/DC.

1975

January – Drummer Peter Clack and bassist Rob Bailey depart. Clack was replaced by Phil Rudd.

January – Bassist Larry Van Kriedt rejoined AC/DC for just a few days after Bailey departed.

February 17 – The Australian only album *High Voltage* was released.

February 24 – The *High Voltage* Australian Tour commenced at Chequers in Sydney.

March – Bassist Mark Evans joined AC/DC.

July – The single 'High Voltage' was released in Australia.

September – Ironically, drummer Colin Burgess temporarily replaced Phil Rudd for a few weeks after the latter injured his hand.

September – The *High Voltage* Australian Tour ended at the International Hotel in Melbourne, Australia.

December – The Australian only album *T.N.T* was released.

1976

January 2 – The *Lock Up Your Daughters* Summer Vacation Tour commenced at the Civic Hall in Portland, Australia.

January 24 – The *Lock Up Your Daughters* Summer Vacation Tour ended at the Memorial Drive in Adelaide, Australia.

March 1 – The single 'T.N.T.' was released in Australia.

April 23 – The *High Voltage* Tour commenced at the Red Cow in London, England.

May 14 – The international version of *High Voltage* was released.

June – The single 'Jailbreak' was released in Australia.

June 4 – AC/DC played their first ever gig at the famed London venue, The Marquee.

September 20 – The Australian version of *Dirty Deeds Done Dirt Cheap* was released.

October 18 – The *High Voltage* Tour ended at the Congresgebouw in Den Haag, Holland.

October – The *Dirty Deeds Done Dirt Cheap* UK Tour commenced at Southampton University, England.

October – The single 'Dirty Deeds Done Dirt Cheap' was released in Australia.

November 15 – The *Dirty Deeds Done Dirt Cheap* UK tour ended at the New Theatre in Oxford, England.

AC/DC

December 17 – The international version of *Dirty Deeds Done Dirt Cheap* was released.

December – The *A Giant Dose Of Rock 'N' Roll* Australian Tour commenced at the Royal Oak Hotel in Richmond, Australia.

December 23 – The *A Giant Dose Of Rock 'N' Roll* Australian Tour ended at the Miami High School Greta Hall in Gold Coast, Australia.

1977

January – The single 'Dirty Deeds Done Dirt Cheap' was released in the UK.

January – The single 'Love At First Feel' was released in Australia.

February 18 – The *Dirty Deeds Done Dirt Cheap* UK Tour commenced at Edinburgh University in Edinburgh, Scotland.

March 20 – The *Dirty Deeds Done Dirt Cheap* UK Tour ended at the Greyhound in Croydon, England.

March 21 – The Australian version of *Let There Be Rock* was released.

March – The single 'Whole Lotta Rosie' was released in Australia.

April 3 – AC/DC performed live on the Aussie TV pop show *Countdown* hosted by Molly Meldrum.

April 5 – AC/DC supported Black Sabbath on a tour of Europe beginning at the Pavillon de Paris in France.

April 22 – The tour with Black Sabbath finished at the Scandinavium in Goteborg, Sweden.

May 27 – Reportedly the date when AC/DC asked bassist Cliff Williams to join the band.

June 23 – The international version of *Let There Be Rock* was released.

June 23 – The single 'Whole Lotta Rosie' was released internationally.

July 27 – The *Let There Be Rock* tour commenced at the Armadillo World Headquarters in Austin, Texas, USA.

October – The single 'Let There Be Rock' was released in Australia.

December 7 – The band played a show at the Atlantic Recording Studios in NYC, which was recorded and released as *Live From The Atlantic Studios*.

December 21 – The *Let There Be Rock* Tour ended at the Stanley Theatre in Pittsburgh, USA.

1978

April 27 – The *Powerage* Tour commenced at the Victoria Hall in Henley, England.

May 25 – *Powerage* was released.

June – The single 'Rock 'N' Roll Damnation' was released in Australia.

October 13 – *If You Want Blood… You've Got It* was released.

AC/DC

October 27 – The *Powerage* Tour ended at the Koekelaarse Sporthal in Koekelare in Belgium.

October 28 – The *If You Want Blood* Tour commenced at the University of Essex in Essex, England.

1979

July 13 – The *Highway To Hell* Tour commenced at the Rijnhal in Arnhem, Holland.

July 27 – *Highway To Hell* was released.

July – 'Highway To Hell' was released as a single in the UK.

August 5 – The *If You Want Blood* Tour ended at the Spectrum Arena in Philadelphia, USA.

December 9 – The band played a show at the Pavillon de Paris in France which was recorded and released as *Let There Be Rock: The Movie – Live In Paris*.

1980

January 27 – The *Highway To Hell* Tour ended at the Gaumont in Southampton, England. It was Bon Scott's last live performance

February 19 – Bon Scott died.

March – Singer Brian Johnson auditioned in London for AC/DC.

April 1 – The news that Brian Johnson was the new singer in AC/DC was made official.

July 25 – Brian Johnson's debut *Back In Black* was released.

BIBLIOGRAPHY
& SOURCES

ACKNOWLEDGEMENTS

Thanks to the following rockers for making this book possible: Al Atkins, Geoff Barton, Jerry Bloom, R. Scott Bolton, Anthony Bozza, Tom Beaujour, Mick Box, Brian Boyd, Paul Cashmere, Rob Cavuoto, Alan Di Perna, Malcolm Dome, Doro, Arnaud Durieux, Mark Evans, Rob Evans, Jeff Gilbert, Colin Hart, Tim Henderson, Magnus Henriksson, Thom Jennings, Scott Kara, Bruce Kulick, Kathy McCabe, Joel McIver, Markus Muller, John Parks, Martin Popoff, Mark Prindle, Scott Redeker, Martin Roach and Independent Music Press, Steven Rosen, Barry Spencer Scrannage, Sylvie Simmons, Darryl Sterdan, Phil Sutcliffe, Jacqui Swift, Brian Tatler, Clinton Walker, K.S. Wang and Jeb Wright.

The author would like to express his gratitude to the following people who were kindly interviewed either for this book and/or for the author's previous work, which has been extremely useful for this book: Jerry Bloom, Mick Box, Jake Brown, Malcolm Dome, Doro, Arnaud Durieux, Mark Evans, Rob Evans, Colin Hart, Bruce Kulick, Mike Newdeck, Martin Popoff, Phil Sutcliffe, Brian Tatler and Clinton Walker. You rock!

AC/DC

Also, the author would like to thank Mick Box of Uriah Heep for supplying a Foreword as well as Bruce Kulick, formally of KISS and now of Grand Funk Railroad, and the German heavy metal legend Doro Pesch for providing Afterwords. You guys rock!

Thank you to the following journalists whose published work was extremely helpful in researching this book: Billy Altman, Geoff Barton, Tom Beaujour, Richard Bienstock, R. Scott Bolton, Brian Boyd, Paul Cashmere, Rob Cavuoto, Robert Christgau, Stephen Thomas Erlewine, David Fricke, Jeff Gilbert, Tim Henderson, Tim Holmes, Thom Jennings, Scott Kara, Dale Kawashima, Gret Kot, Jim Ladd, Dave Ling, Kurt Loder, Dan Marsicano, Kathy McCabe, John Parks, Alan Di Perna, Alexis Petridis, Greg Prato, Mark Prindle, Scott Redeker, Eduardo Rivadavia, Steven Rosen, Greg Sandow, Sylvie Simmons, Darryl Sterdan, Phil Sutcliffe, Jacqui Swift, K.S. Wang and Jeb Wright.

Special thanks to Phil Sutcliffe and Brian Tatler, as well as John Tucker. Apologies for those names that I'm bound to have forgotten. Also thanks to my parents, Ann and Andrew, my family and good friends, Scott, Rob, Ste, Dave and Graeme.

Visit *www.neildaniels.com* and *neildanielsbooks.wordpress.com* for details on my other books.

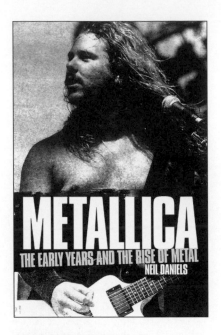

METALLICA
THE EARLY YEARS
AND THE RISE OF METAL
by Neil Daniels

This is the first and only book to look at the massive impact of Metallica's first four albums on the international metal scene. This book tells the story of how Metallica's remarkable global triumph started, complete with examples of very early memorabilia and exclusive interviews from people who saw those early gigs and can provide eye-witness accounts of this incredible story.

ISBN: 978-1-906191-21-4 Paperback, 208 Pages including b/w pics, 234x153mm World Rights £12.99

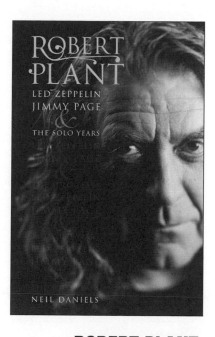

ROBERT PLANT:
LED ZEPPELIN, JIMMY PAGE & THE
SOLO YEARS
by Neil Daniels

The first and only complete biography of this genuine rock legend including all solo work post-Led Zeppelin. Told in its entirety for the very first time, this is the story of an enthusiastic young kid from the West Midlands who adored his humble blues roots and defied his stern parents by becoming one of the world's most recognisable and iconic rock superstars. This biography brings his career bang up-to-date, covering his latest album *Raising Sand* with the revered bluegrass singer Alison Krauss and the highly-publicised Led Zeppelin reunion in December, 2007.

For the first time, his solo years, his recordings with his former Led Zep cohort Jimmy Page and numerous guest appearances are covered in depth in a complete rock biography. The author also delves into Plant's earliest and ongoing influences and passions such as Southern American blues and classic fifties R&B; the book also places Plant's later work in the wider context of both Led Zep's own legacy and the broader history of modern music.

ISBN 978-0-9552822-7-0 224 Pages, Paperback, 1x8 pgs b/w pics
234x153mm, World Rights £12.99

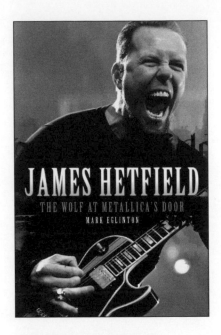

JAMES HETFIELD:
THE WOLF AT METALLICA'S DOOR
by Mark Eglinton

The first and only biography of Hetfield, frontman of the biggest rock band of the modern era. Hetfield's overwhelming presence has always guided Metallica's every dramatic step. However, behind the scenes was a complex band fronted by a genius who had his own personal battle to fight – throwing the future of Metallica into considerable doubt. His subsequent re-emergence as a re-invented rock legend is a personal and professional triumph. Author and Metallica expert Mark Eglinton has compiled an exhaustive array of exclusive and first-hand interviews from key players in the story, and in so doing has constructed the definitive biography on Metallica's frontman.

ISBN: 978-1-906191-04-7 Paperback, 208 Pages including 1x8 pages b/w pics, 234x153mm World Rights £12.99

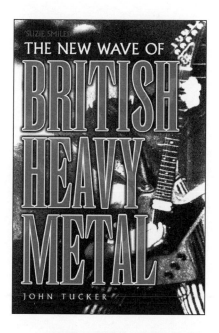

THE NEW WAVE OF BRITISH HEAVY METAL
SUZIE SMILED
by John Tucker

This book tells the definitive and complete history of the NWOBHM, from its formation during the late 1970s, through its numerous peaks and troughs in the 1980s and on to its current status as one of rock music's most influential genres. The most famous exponents of this New Wave are stadium-selling acts such as Motörhead, Def Leppard and the currently-enormous-again Iron Maiden, but there are also scores of other acts who have been selling millions of records to the movement's enormous fan-base for years.

Suzie Smiled ... describes what it was like to be writing and playing heavy metal in the post-punk era and sets the music in the bleak social context of the time. This book is the first ever collection of stories from the bands of the NWOBHM. Through a mixture of exclusive new interviews, contemporary articles and unpublished photographs, *Suzie Smiled*... lets the musicians tell the story, including how some of the greatest heavy metal songs ever written were created.

ISBN 978-0-9549704-7-5 256 Pages
234x153mm, Paperback, 1x8 pags b/w pics, World Rights £12.99